W9-CIJ-962

U·X·L newsmakers

volume **6** six

L–Y

Carol Brennan,
Kelle S. Sisung,
Rebecca Valentine

Sarah Hermsen, *Project Editor*

THOMSON
GALE

Detroit • New York • San Francisco • San Diego • New Haven, Conn. • Waterville, Maine • London • Munich

U•X•L Newsmakers, Volume 6

Carol Brennan, Kelle S. Sisung, and Rebecca Valentine

Project Editor
Sarah Hermsen

Rights Acquisition and Management
Ron Montgomery

Imaging and Multimedia
Dean Dauphinais, Mike Logusz

Product Design
Kate Scheible

Composition and Electronic Prepress
Evi Seoud

Manufacturing
Rita Wimberley

For permission to use material from this product, submit your request via Web at http://www.gale-edit.com/permissions, or you may download our Permissions Request form and submit your request by fax or mail to:

Rights Acquisition and Management Department
Thomson Gale
27500 Drake Rd.
Farmington Hills, MI 48331-3535
Permissions Hotline:
248-699-8006 or 800-877-4253, ext. 8006
Fax: 248-699-8074 or 800-762-4058

While every effort has been made to ensure the reliability of the information presented in this publication, Thomson Gale does not guarantee the accuracy of data contained herein. Thomson Gale accepts no payment for listing; and inclusion in the publication of any organization, agency, institution, publication, service, or individual does not imply endorsement by the editors or publisher. Errors brought to the attention of the publisher and verified to the satisfaction of the publisher will be corrected in future editions.

ISBN 0-7876-9189-5 (set, vols. 1–4)
ISBN 0-7876-9190-9 (v. 1)
ISBN 0-7876-9191-7 (v. 2)
ISBN 0-7876-9194-1 (v. 3)
ISBN 0-7876-9195-X (v. 4)
ISBN 1-4144-0155-8 (set, vols. 5–6)
ISBN 1-4144-0156-6 (v. 5)
ISBN 1-4144-0157-4 (v. 6)

ISSN 1557-6760

This title is also available as an e-book.
ISBN 1-4144-0493-X
Contact your Thomson Gale sales representative for ordering information.

Printed in the United States of America
10 9 8 7 6 5 4 3 2 1

contents

u·x·l newsmakers · *volume 6* · by field of endeavor

Entertainment

Government

Music

Religion

Science

Social Issues

Sports

Writing

U ·*X·L Newsmakers* is the place to turn for information on personalities active on the current scene. Containing fifty biographies, *U·X·L Newsmakers* covers contemporary figures who are making headlines in a variety of fields, including entertainment, government, literature, music, pop culture, science, and sports. Subjects include international figures, as well as people of diverse ethnic backgrounds.

Format

Biographies are arranged alphabetically across two volumes. Each entry opens with the individual's birth date, place of birth, and field of endeavor. Entries provide readers with information on the early life, influences, and career of the individual or group being profiled. Most entries feature one or more photographs of the subject, and all entries provide a list of sources for further reading about the individual or group. Readers may also locate entries by using the Field of Endeavor table of contents listed in the front of each volume, which lists biographees by vocation.

Features

- A Field of Endeavor table of contents, found at the front of each volume, allows readers to access the biographees by the category for which they are best known. Categories include: Art/Design, Business, Entertainment, Government, Music, Science, Social Issues, Sports, and Writing. When applicable, subjects are listed under more than one category for even greater access.

- Sidebars include information relating to the biographee's career and activities (for example, writings, awards, life milestones), brief biographies of related individuals, and explanations of movements, groups, and more, connected with the person.

- Quotes from and about the biographee offer insight into their lives and personal philosophies.

- More than 100 black-and-white photographs are featured across the volumes.

- Sources for more information, including books, magazine articles, and Web sites, are provided at the end of each entry.

- A comprehensive and cumulative subject index quickly points readers to the people and subjects discussed in all six volumes of *U•X•L Newsmakers*.

Comments and Suggestions

The individuals chosen for these volumes were drawn from all walks of life and from across a variety of professions. Many names came directly from the headlines of the day, while others were selected with the interests of students in mind. By no means is the list exhaustive. Suggestions for subjects to be profiled in future volumes of *U•X•L Newsmakers* as well as comments on this work itself should be sent to: Editor, *U•X•L Newsmakers,* U•X•L, 27500 Drake Road, Farmington Hills, Michigan 48331-3535; call toll-free: 1-800-877-4253; or send an e-mail via www.gale.com.

U·X·L newsmakers

Shia LaBeouf

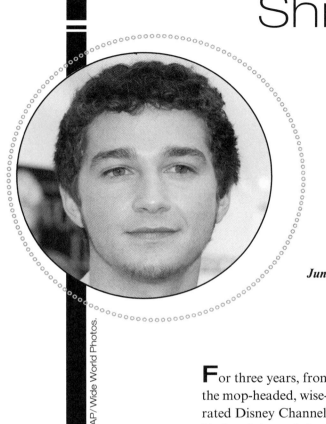

June 11, 1986 • *Los Angeles, California*

Actor

For three years, from 2000 until 2003, most people knew him as the mop-headed, wise-cracking younger brother Louis on the top-rated Disney Channel series *Even Stevens*. But in 2003, thanks to his breakthrough lead role in the movie *Holes,* teen actor Shia LaBeouf made an almost seamless transition from the small screen to the big screen. That same year LaBeouf appeared in no fewer than three other movies, taking small roles in *Dumb and Dumberer* and *Charlie's Angels: Full Throttle,* and starring in the acclaimed HBO show *The Battle of Shaker Heights*. It seemed LaBeouf was everywhere. He garnered praise from surprised critics, who called him an up-and-comer to watch. *Teen People* placed him firmly on their Young Hollywood Hot List in 2004, and his fan base grew broader by the minute. There was no stopping LaBeouf, who went on to costar in the 2005 blockbuster *Constantine* and to play American golf icon Francis Ouimet in *The Greatest Game Ever Played* (2005). In less than two years LaBeouf transformed from cheeky child performer to an adult star to be reckoned with.

Young Cajun cutup

Like many young entertainers, Shia (pronounced SHI-yuh) Shaide LaBeouf comes from a showbiz family. He was born on June 11, 1986, in Los Angeles, California, the only child of Jeffrey and Shayna LaBeouf. At various times Jeffrey was employed as a comedian, a rodeo clown, and a performer in a circus, where it was his job to train chickens. Shayna was a former ballet dancer who eventually turned to designing clothing and jewelry. When the couple had their son they named him Shia after Shayna's father, who was a Jewish comedian; Shia means "gift from God" in Hebrew.

"It's not like I'm Mahatma Gandhi. I'm just a kid from the Disney Channel."

In interviews LaBeouf claims that his Jewish mom and Cajun dad encouraged him to speak his mind from an early age. He took their encouragement to heart and began performing comedy routines at the age of three in the LaBeouf living room. As he told *People* in 2003, "I'd do five minutes on how crazy our life was, like how at Thanksgiving we'd have matzo gumbo or spicy gefilte." (Gefilte is a traditional Jewish dish; it is a type of seasoned fish.) By the age of twelve the precocious youngster was doing stand-up at local coffeehouses; he also landed a gig at the Ice House Comedy Club in Pasadena. In the same *People* article, LaBeouf explained that his material was "really dirty and gross," and "definitely not Disneyesque."

After getting a taste of the spotlight LaBeouf decided he wanted to branch out into acting, especially after a friend of his began appearing on the television drama *Dr. Quinn, Medicine Woman*. The industrious thirteen-year-old pulled out the telephone book, found the name of an acting agent, and auditioned by performing one of his stand-up routines. The agent signed him immediately and sent LaBeouf on his first casting calls.

Likeable Louis

Unlike most entertainers just starting out, LaBeouf did not have to endure hundreds of disappointing rejections. In fact, on one of his very first auditions he snagged a leading role on a new comedy series on the Disney Channel called *Even Stevens,* which centered around an upper-middle-class family living in Sacramento, California. Dad was an attorney; Mom was a state senator. Older son, Donnie, was a high school sports star; and Ren was the ideal daughter. That left the youngest son, Louis, the class clown who was less than perfect and who struggled to fit in with his perfect family.

With his easy grin, quick timing, and just the right touch of geekiness, LaBeouf was the perfect Louis. And, although the show was initially supposed to feature the entire family, it soon became apparent that Christy Romano (1984–) as Ren and LaBeouf as Louis were the program's true stars. When *Even Stevens* premiered in June 2003, Carole Horst of *Variety* gave it a tentative thumbs up, but she had nothing but praise for Romano and LaBeouf. According to Horst, they "should start plotting the rest of their careers, as these two young thesps [actors] bring polish and excellent timing to the material." Viewers agreed with the critics, and soon *Even Stevens* became the highest-rated daytime show on the Disney Channel. Over the next three seasons LaBeouf continued to be prominently featured, and he increasingly drew more and more fans of all ages. In 2003, when he was just sixteen, LaBeouf snagged a Daytime Emmy Award for Outstanding Performer in a Children's Series. (Daytime Emmies are awarded each year to honor excellence in all forms of daytime television production.)

A "Hole" lotta luck

Even Stevens was cancelled in 2003, but the lucky LaBeouf was not without a job for long. Competing against hundreds of other hopefuls, he auditioned for the Disney major motion-picture release of *Holes.* The movie is based on the enormously popular children's book of the same name written in 1998 by Louis Sachar (1954–). Director Andrew Davis had never seen an episode of *Even Stevens,* but he still tapped the talented LaBeouf to play the main character of both the book and movie, Stanley Yelnats. Stanley is wrongfully convicted of stealing and is sent to a juvenile detention camp called Camp Green Lake, where all the detainees are forced to dig holes in the blistering desert heat.

Before the film began shooting, LaBeouf and cast spent two weeks going through a training camp where they climbed ropes, did countless push-ups, and, of course, dug holes. Although the physical preparation was tough, in interviews LaBeouf said he was glad for the experience because it got him in shape to work in 105-degree heat; plus it gave him a chance to bond with the rest of the actors. The young stars also became tight because they attended school together in air-conditioned trailers on the set. As LaBeouf laughingly told Marie Morreale of *Scholastic News,* it "was the only time in my life where I ran to school because I was getting air-conditioning and water."

Author Louis Sachar also wrote the screenplay and was on the set every day providing pointers. He and LaBeouf became especially good friends, and as LaBeouf expressed in several interviews, he found the writer to be an "intriguing and knowledgeable character." An ironic twist is that LaBeouf had not read *Holes* before taking the role of Stanley, but he was assigned to read the book for school during the shooting of the film.

Given the green light

Holes was released in April 2003 to a great deal of critical acclaim. But LaBeouf was just getting started. In June 2003 he had small roles in two more big-screen offerings: the comedy *Dumb and Dumberer: When Harry Met Lloyd* and the action-adventure *Charlie's Angels: Full Throttle.* His next big hit, however, came on the small screen when he took the lead in the HBO-Project Greenlight original movie *The Battle of Shaker Heights.* Project Greenlight is a production company started by friends-turned-screenwriters-turned-actors Ben Affleck (1972–) and Matt Damon (1970–) to support and encourage other aspiring writers.

Shaker Heights is a coming-of-age story that focuses on seventeen-year-old Kelly Ernswiler, whose primary passion in

Shia LaBeouf garnered glowing reviews for his performance in the 2005 film Constantine, *costarring Keanu Reeves and Djimon Hounsou.* © David James/ Warner Bros/Zuma/Corbis.

life is participating in war reenactments. Part of his attraction to fantasy life is that his shaky confidence makes him a target for bullies at school; Kelly must also cope with the illness of his father, who is an ex-drug addict. LaBeouf dug into own past to tap into Kelly's troubled emotions: His father Jeffrey battled a drug addiction for several years while he was growing up.

The movie was originally broadcast in August 2003, but it received only lukewarm reviews. Frank Scheck of the *Hollywood Reporter* claimed it felt "choppy and unfocused," especially since it tended to veer "sharply back and forth between broad comedy and heartfelt drama, ultimately succeeding on neither level." LaBeouf, however, was singled out as the film's one bright spot. According to Scheck, "The character [of Kelly] is superbly realized by LaBeouf, who balances the role's comedic and emotional demands and whose screen presence always commands attention."

Francis Ouimet: Unlikely American Hero

When twenty-year-old Francis Ouimet won the 1913 U.S. Open, he became the youngest player and first amateur to take home the top prize in the country's most prestigious golf contest. He not only made sports history, but proved that the American dream was truly obtainable.

Francis Desales Ouimet was born on May 8, 1893, in Brookline, Massachusetts, the youngest son of Louis and Mary Ellen Ouimet. Ouimet's father, a French Canadian immigrant, was a gardener, and as luck would have it, he moved his family to a house situated just across the street from the Brookline Country Club, one of the oldest and most prestigious private golf clubs in the United States. At the time, golf was a sport of the privileged class, which meant that working-class people like the Ouimets did not play. Francis's older brother, Wilfred, however, became a caddy (person hired by a golfer to carry golf clubs), and when he was not working the younger Ouimet would steal a club and hit balls in the cow pasture behind their house.

When he was eleven years old Ouimet became a caddy like his brother and was soon hooked on the game. He often got up at 5:00 AM and played on the Brookline course until he was chased off by the greens-keepers. While attending Brookline High he formed the school's first golf team, and by 1909 the young swinger was the Greater Boston Interscholastic Champion. In 1910, 1911, and 1912, Ouimet tried to qualify for the National Amateur Championships, but failed. In 1913, he had better luck at the state level and scored as the Massachusetts Amateur Champion. To pay for his tournament fees and equipment Ouimet took a job at a local sporting goods store.

That same year, the U.S. Open was being played at Brookline Country Club. In a surprising turn, Ouimet was asked to fill a last-minute spot by Robert Watson, president of the U. S. Golf Association. At first Ouimet was reluctant, especially since he did not want to take time off work. But he assumed he would lose quickly, plus the opportunity to meet two of his heroes, legendary British players Harry Vardon (1870–1937)

Swings into adult roles

In 2003, sandwiched between film releases, LaBeouf somehow managed to graduate from high school. He told interviewers that he planned to attend college in the future, but in the meantime he was just too busy. As LaBeouf told Fred Topel of *about.com,* "I just wanted to work and get jobs at first. Now I get to be picky and have fun." Being picky allowed the teenager to join the cast of such blockbusters as 2004's *I, Robot,* a science fiction thriller starring one of LaBeouf's idols, Will Smith (1968–).

In 2005 LaBeouf costarred in *Constantine* with another of his favorite actors, Keanu Reeves (1964–). Based on the and Ted Ray (1877–1914), was too tempting to pass up.

Ouimet started off poorly, but he quickly gained confidence thanks to his firsthand knowledge of the course. By the September 19 playoffs he was neck-and-neck with Vardon and Ray, and on September 20, 1913, he pulled ahead, beating Vardon by six strokes and Ray by five. The victory made Ouimet an unexpected American sports hero. At twenty years old, he was the youngest player ever to win the U.S. Open, and the first amateur. Ouimet was also an unlikely celebrity, considering he was a very gawky young man—beanpole thin with ears that stuck out.

Although he became a stockbroker in 1919, Ouimet remained an amateur golfer the rest of his life, winning a number of championships both in the United States and abroad. He is considered to be the player who brought the game of golf to the masses. In 1913, approximately 350,000 Americans were golfers; ten years later that number had increased to two million. In 1949, at the age of fifty-six, Ouimet retired from amateur golf, but not from the sport. That same year he also established a college scholarship fund for caddies. Admired by

Francis Ouimet. Hulton Archive/Getty Images.

his peers as a cool-headed and modest player until the end, Ouimet died in 1967 in Newton, Massachusetts.

Hell-blazer series of DC/Vertigo graphic novels, the movie centers on the exploits of a supernatural detective named John Constantine, played by Reeves. LaBeouf plays Constantine's sidekick, Chas, who, according to Sarah Wilson of *Interview,* is a "bighearted, overeager demon slayer in the making." The movie fared well with fans of the original series and there was immediate talk of a sequel. In general, though, most of the praise went to LaBeouf, who provided the few glimpses of comic relief in the dark thriller. Wilson claimed that the fledgling actor stole scene after scene from Reeves. And, according to Peter Travers of *Rolling Stone,* LaBeouf turned in one "juicy" supporting performance."

By mid-2005, with several standout performances under his belt, the eighteen-year-old LaBeouf seemed ready to tackle his first significant, grown-up role. That chance quickly came when he nabbed the lead in *The Greatest Game Ever Played.* Released in September of 2005 *The Greatest Game* chronicles the life of Francis Ouimet, an almost forgotten golf legend who, at the age of twenty, became the first amateur (and the youngest player) to ever win the U.S. Open, a major golf tournament. LaBeouf trained for over six months to perfect his swing, sometimes playing golf for almost six hours a day. He also toured with the University of California Los Angeles golf team and worked with several professional trainers. As he boasted to Rob Allstetter of the *Detroit News,* "Nobody has trained (in golf) like this for a film. And there's no swing like this on film I don't think—ever."

Hotter than ever

Many predicted that his role as Ouimet would be LaBeouf's breakthrough performance, cementing him on the short list of performers who successful made the transition from child star to adult actor. And, in clips heralding the release of *The Greatest Game,* audiences were given a glimpse of a young man on the brink of being grown up—taller, leaner, and with a newly shorn haircut. Jessica Blatt of *CosmoGIRL!* commented, "He's always been hilarious and adorable.... Now he's hotter than ever in Hollywood."

Blatt also observed that the young star known for his wisecracking both on screen and off was also pretty deep and "whip-smart." When asked what it was like to be a celebrity, LaBeouf replied, "Celebrity has a different meaning from actor. I have respect for the word actor.... My ultimate goal is to be the most respected actor on the planet, not the most famous celebrity." Perhaps, however, LaBeouf may switch to directing. In his spare time he enjoys making short films, one of which is about a boy who has a lobster for a pet. But whether LaBeouf chooses to stick it out in Hollywood remains to be seen. As he admitted to Blatt, "I don't know if I want to be a director forever or an actor forever, but I just love film. Even before I was in this business, all I ever did was watch movies."

For More Information

Periodicals

"The Ace in Holes." *People* (May 19, 2003): p. 128.

Blatt, Jessica. "Shia LaBeouf Grows Up." *CosmoGIRL!* (March 2005): pp. 174–76.

Horst, Carole. "Young Leads Shine in Sibling Sitcom." *Variety* (June 19, 2000) p. 35.

Scheck, Frank. "'Battle of Shaker Heights' Review." *Hollywood Reporter* (August 23, 2003): p. 12.

Wilson, Sarah. "Shia LaBeouf: His Latest Role Has Him Battling for the Souls of Humanity—and Stealing Scenes from Keanu Reeves." *Interview* (March 2005): p. 100.

Web Sites

Allstetter, Rob. "Talking With ... Shia LaBeouf." *Detroit News: Sports Insider* (February 16, 2005). http://www.detnews.com/2005/golf/0502/16/G04-91013.htm (accessed on August 23, 2005).

Even Stevens Online. http://evenstevens.disneytvzone.com/evenstevens/welcome/launcher.html (accessed on August 23, 2005).

Fischer, Paul. "Interview: Shia LaBeouf 'Constantine.'" *Dark Horizons.* (February 8, 2005). http://www.darkhorizons.com/news05/constan3.php (accessed on August 23, 2005).

Morreale, Marie. "Holes Is Definitely Worth Checking Out, Says Shia LaBeouf." *Scholastic News.* http://teacher.scholastic.com/scholasticnews/indepth/holes/Stanley.htm (accessed on August 23, 2005).

"Shia LaBeouf Biography." *Kidzworld.com.* http://www.kidzworld.com/site/p3813.htm (accessed on August 23, 2005).

Takagaki, Sarah. "Shia LaBeouf, Actor." *TimeforKids.com* (April 16, 2003). http://www.timeforkids.com/TFK/kidscoops/story/0,14989,444229,00.html (accessed on August 23, 2005).

Topel, Fred. "Shia LaBeouf Interview." *about.com: Action-Adventure Movies* (August 22, 2003). http://actionadventure.about.com/cs/weeklystories/a/aa082203.htm (accessed on August 23, 2003).

Travers, Peter. "Review of *Constantine.*" *Rolling Stone* (February 17, 2005). http://www.rollingstone.com/reviews/movie/_/id/6153709?pageid=rs.ReviewsMovieArchive&pageregion=mainRegion&rnd=1120954283120&has-player=true&version=6.0.8.1024 (accessed on August 23, 2005).

Avril Lavigne

September 27, 1984 • *Belleville, Ontario,*
Canada

Singer, songwriter

In 2002 an eighteen-year-old Canadian newcomer named Avril Lavigne swept on to the U.S. music scene with her debut disc, *Let Go*. By the end of the year, three singles from the album, including "Complicated," broke into the top ten of the Billboard charts, and *Let Go* was the second best-selling CD of the year. Lavigne's music scored high with fans and critics, but so did her personal style, which consisted of wearing loose pants, tank tops, and neckties. As a result, she sparked a fashion trend and was heralded in the press as a "skater-punk," an alternative to pop princesses, like Britney Spears (1981–), whose look and videos had started to become increasingly more provocative. In May 2004 Lavigne released her second album, *Under My Skin,* which debuted at number one not only in the United States, but also in many other countries, including Germany, Spain, and Japan. By the end of 2005 Avrilmania was showing no signs of slowing—Lavigne was performing to sold-out crowds on an extended concert tour and in April she took home top honors at the Juno Awards, which are considered to be the Canadian equivalent of the U.S. Grammy Awards.

Not a girlie-girl

Avril Ramona Lavigne was born on September 27, 1984, in Belleville, a small city in the eastern part of the province of Ontario, Canada. The second of three children, her father, John, was a technician for Bell Canada; mother Judy was a

"Why should I care what other people think of me? I am who I am. And who I wanna be."

stay-at-home mom. When Lavigne was five, the family moved to Napanee, a farming town even smaller than Belleville with a total population of only five thousand. From the time she was a toddler Lavigne idolized her older brother, Matt, and insisted on trying to do anything he could do. As she explained to Chris Willman of *Entertainment Weekly,* "If he played hockey, I had to play hockey. He played baseball, I wanted to." In fact, when Lavigne was ten she played in the Napanee boy's hockey league; she also became known as quite a baseball pitcher.

As she grew older Lavigne gained a reputation as a tomboy who preferred family outings like dirt biking or camping over dating. And in the tenth grade she discovered skateboarding, which became a particular passion. "I'm just not a girlie-girl," Lavigne laughingly told Willman. When not playing sports, however, she did pursue another interest—singing. The Lavignes were devout Christians and attended Evangel Temple in Napanee, where young Avril sang in the choir beginning at age ten. Soon she branched out and began singing at all types of venues, including county fairs, hockey games, and company parties. She primarily sang covers of songs made popular by country singers Martina McBride (1966–) and Faith Hill (1967–). Lavigne's parents bought her a sound machine to sing along with, and she practiced in front of a mirror at home for hours.

In 1998, when she was fourteen years old, Lavigne's first manager, Cliff Fabri, discovered her singing at a small performance in a local bookstore. When talking to Willman, Fabri described the young girl as a "frizzy-haired waif." But he liked Lavigne's voice, and he was especially impressed by her confident attitude. That same year, such confidence helped her win a contest to sing a duet with fellow Canadian Shania Twain (1965–) at the jam-packed Corel Centre in Ottawa. Even though it was her first time performing in front of twenty thousand people, Lavigne was fearless. As she told Willman, "I thought, 'This is what I'm going to do with my life.'"

Lavigne lets go

Two years later, when she was sixteen, Fabri arranged for Lavigne to audition for L.A. Reid, head of Arista Records in New York City. After a fifteen-minute tryout Reid signed Lavigne to an amazing two-record, $1.25 million contract. The sixteen year old immediately dropped out of high school to devote herself to working on her first album. At first producers offered Lavigne new country tunes to sing, but after six months the team was unable to write any actual songs, and it became apparent that things were not clicking. Reid then sent the singer to Los Angeles to work with a team of producers and writers known as The Matrix. When Lavigne arrived in L.A. Matrix producer Lauren Christy asked Lavigne what style she had in mind. As Christy relayed to Chris Willman, Lavigne had responded, "I'm 16. I want to rock out." That same day Lavigne and Matrix writers penned the first song for her album, "Complicated."

Lavigne's debut album, *Let Go,* was released on June 4, 2002, and within six weeks it had gone platinum, meaning over a million copies were sold. The single "Complicated," which received a great deal of radio airplay, reached number one on the adult Billboard charts; "I'm With You" also reached number one on the adult charts; and the catchy pop tune "Sk8er Boi" was

With edgy lyrics and a strong voice, Avril Lavigne has become one of America's top-selling entertainers. AP/Wide World Photos.

a top-requested video on MTV and made it in the top ten of the Billboard Hot 100.

To promote the album Lavigne set out on a whirlwind publicity tour, making appearances on talk shows such as *Late Night with David Letterman,* and giving a series of concerts in Europe with her newly formed band, which was put together by her new management firm, Nettwerk. Most inexperienced singers are backed by seasoned musicians, but Nettwerk chose to go with young performers who were up and coming in the Canadian punk-rock scene. As Nettwerk manager Shauna Gold told

Shanda Deziel of *Maclean's,* "[Lavigne] is young, her music's young, we needed a band that would fit well with who she is as a person."

And, after being away from her small-town home in Canada, Lavigne was beginning to form her own personal style. Initially publicists tried to market her like other teen pop stars, but Lavigne rebelled. "If I was made up by the record label," she remarked to Lorraine Ali of *Newsweek,* "I'd have bleached-blonde hair and I'd probably be wearing a bra for a shirt." Instead, the singer-songwriter opted for a skater-punk look, which consisted of cut-off plaid pants, steel-toed Doc Martens, and tank tops worn with neckties. According to Ali, the five-foot-one tomboy "spawned a prepubescent army of Lavignettes" who snatched up her records and faithfully copied her outfits.

Finds independence with *Under My Skin*

By the end of 2002 *Let Go* had sold 4.9 million copies and was the second best-seller of the year just behind *The Eminem Show.* (By 2005 worldwide sales topped over fourteen million.) As 2003 progressed Lavigne continued to gather more fame and more accolades. She performed to sold-out crowds at her first North American concert tour; nabbed five Grammy nominations, including Song of the Year for "I'm With You"; and was named Best New Artist at the MTV Video Music Awards. In Canada Lavigne received six Juno nominations, winning four, including Best New Artist and Best Pop Album.

In the press Lavigne was deemed the leader of the pack of a new group of edgy, female singer-songwriters, which included Pink (1979–) and Michelle Branch (1983–). She also endured being called the "anti-Britney," referring to Britney Spears. In interviews Lavigne expressed her distaste for the label. "I don't like that term," she told Chris Willman. "It's stupid. She's a human being. God, leave her alone." But, in the same interview radio programmer Tom Poleman explained to Willman that Lavigne's popularity was partly thanks to her "anti-Britney" style. "Avril is much more the regular kid," Poleman commented.

Canadian Punk Rockers: Sum 41

In June 2005 Avril Lavigne became engaged to her boyfriend of a year, Deryck Whibley (1980–), the lead singer of Canadian punk-pop group called Sum 41, whose members are known for their quick, catchy rock tunes and their highly energized live performances.

Sum 41 is composed of four musicians: drummer Steve "Stevo" Jocz, lead vocalist Deryck "Bizzy D" Whibley, lead guitarist Dave "Brownsound" Baksh, and bass player Jason "Cone" McCaslin. All four attended the same high school in Ajax, Ontario, and all played in various high school bands that performed in and around Toronto. In 1996, during the summer of their junior year, Jocz and Whibley decided to join forces and form their own band; they called it Sum 41 since the group was founded on the forty-first day of summer vacation. Jocz and Whibley tried out a number of bass players and guitarists before asking Baksh and McClasin to join the band. By 1999 the group was cemented and they began to create a unique sound that borrowed from all kinds of music, including hip-hop, heavy metal, and alternative rock.

By late 1999 the foursome had created their own press kit, which included a ten-minute video featuring some of their musical numbers interspersed with clips of the band mates pulling pranks. They sent the kit off to several major record labels, and within a week Sum 41 was signed by Island Records. The band's first album, *Half Hour of Power* (2000), attracted little attention, but with 2001's *All Killer No Filler* Sum 41 began to reach an international fan base, especially because of the hit single "Fat Lip," which reached number sixty-six on the U.S. Billboard charts. The band attracted a loyal fol-lowing (who called themselves the Bomb Squad) particularly because of their on-stage antics. During Sum 41's 2001 Tour of the Rising Sun they pogo-jumped, participated in mock guitar

"For boys, she seems more attainable; girls can see themselves living more like her, dressing the same, being attracted to the same boys."

Despite her hectic schedule Lavigne returned to the studio in 2003 to record her second album, which she was determined to make her own way. Although Lavigne did write several of the songs on *Let Go,* she did so with the help of a slew of producers. This time she flew to Los Angeles to work privately with Canadian singer-songwriter Chantal Kreviazuk (1973–); she also cowrote one song with guitarist Ben Moody (1980–) of the band Evanescence. Lavigne's record label, Arista, did not hear a single track until the newly independent singer was finished. "There was no way I was gonna write songs and send battles, and urged the audience to join in rock song challenges.

The band released two more albums by the mid-2000s: *Does This Look Infected?* (2002) and *Chuck* (2004). The 2004 CD is named after Chuck Pelletier, a United Nations peacekeeper who was instrumental in saving the lives of the band members while they were making a documentary in the Democratic Republic of the Congo (DRC; formerly Zaire). Since the late 1990s the Democratic Republic of Congo had been embroiled in the Second Congo War (1998–2002), a conflict that involved nine African nations, but that was centered in the DRC. Many artists from the United States and Canada have offered humanitarian aid to the citizens of the war-torn country. Although there is tentative peace in the DRC, military threats still exist for civilians. In April 2005 *Chuck* received the Rock Album of the Year prize at the Juno Awards, which are presented annually in Canada to honor achievement in the music industry.

Sum 41. Scott Gries/Getty Images.

them to people to rewrite them like I did last time," Lavigne explained to Lorraine Ali. "I need to feel I'm doing this on my own."

Lavigne's second album, *Under My Skin,* was released on May 25, 2004, and debuted at number one on Billboard's U.S. album chart. It also sparked several popular singles, including "Don't Tell Me" and "My Happy Ending." Critics were consistently kind in their reviews, with Chuck Arnold of *People* applauding Lavigne for her "artistic independence" and praising her "rebellious spirit, racing rhythms, and tough-talking lyrics." Lorraine Ali pointed out that fans were seeing a more mature Lavigne, claiming her new songs "are rougher and darker" and her voice had lost some of its "girly high pitch." One song, in particular, received a good deal of attention—the emotional ballad "Slipped Away," which Lavigne wrote about the death of her grandfather.

Avril's "Happy Ending"

Some of the press surrounding *Under My Skin* came as a result of a twenty-one-city mall tour that Lavigne and her band embarked on just prior to the album's release. As Lavigne explained to Deborah Evans Price of *Billboard*, "We thought it would be cool to put on a free show and give back to the fans." Armies of Lavignettes turned out to demonstrate their support, and thousands of CDs were pre-sold even before the album's release. To encourage even more sales Lavigne again went out on the road doing nonstop interviews and heading out on a spring 2004 concert tour. According to Jill Kipnis of *Billboard*, twenty-six of the thirty-one shows sold out completely and the tour grossed over $9 million.

By the end of 2004 the twenty-year-old Lavigne was the one of America's top-selling entertainers. Her face graced the covers of teen magazines like *CosmoGIRL!*, and she was featured in articles in such national magazines as *Time* and *Newsweek*. She also completed her second sold-out concert tour, the Bonez Tour, which was launched in October. Lavigne ended the year by appearing on the soundtracks of two films, *The Princess Diaries 2: Royal Engagement* and *The SpongeBob SquarePants Movie*.

In 2005, just three years after her debut album appeared, Lavigne was again the top-honored entertainer at Canada's Juno Awards. She received five nominations and took home three prizes, including the Best Artist award and a second win for Best Pop Album. Lavigne also announced that she would be adventuring more into film by lending her voice to a character in an animated movie called *Over the Hedge,* scheduled for a 2006 release. Perhaps the biggest bit of personal Lavigne news came in June 2005, when the Canadian "punk princess" became engaged to boyfriend Deryck Whibley (1980–), lead singer of the Canadian punk-rock group Sum 41.

Although she had only two albums under her belt, most music critics predicted that Avril Lavigne had a solid future. As *USA Today* correspondent Brian Mansfield told *Billboard,* "Avril's core audience may be a very young one, but she strikes me as the type of artist that a wide range of people respect and hope to see succeed. Those are the kind of artists who have long careers."

For More Information

Periodicals

Ali, Lorraine. "Anarchy on MTV? Tough Gals, Rejoice. Scrappy Skater Avril Lavigne Leads the Anti-Britney Revolution." *Newsweek* (December 30, 2002): p. 78.

Ali, Lorraine. "Nobody's Fool: Avril Lavigne Interview." *Newsweek* (March 22, 2004): p. 58.

Arnold, Chuck. "Under My Skin: Avril Lavigne." *People* (May 31, 2004): p. 45.

Burton, Rebecca Brown. "Q&A with Avril Lavigne." *Time* (May 31, 2004): p. 87.

Deziel, Shanda. "Avril's Edge." Maclean's (January 13, 2003): p. 22.

Kipnis, Jill. "Organizers Hope Lavigne Trek Has Happy Ending." *Billboard* (October 30, 2004): p. 16.

Mayfield, Geoff. "'Under' Puts Avril on Top." *Billboard* (June 12, 2004): p. 61.

Price, Deborah Evans. "Avril Goes Back to Basics: Mall Tour Kicks Off Album Publicity Blast." *Billboard* (May 22, 2004) pp. 1–4.

"Usher and Avril: Teen Vogue Celebrates Two on Top of Their Music." *PR Newswire* (October 12, 2004).

Willman, Chris. "Avril Lavigne: The Anti-Britney." *Entertainment Weekly* (November 1, 2002): p. 22.

Web Sites

Avril Lavigne Web Site. http://www.avrillavigne.com (accessed on August 23, 2005).

Sum 41 Web Site. http://www.islandrecords.com/sum41/site/home.las (accessed on August 23, 2005).

Wangari Maathai

April 1, 1940 • *Nyeri, Kenya*

Human rights activist, environmentalist

In 2004 Wangari Maathai became an internationally recognized figure by becoming the first black woman and the first environmentalist to receive the Nobel Peace Prize. Her honor, however, did not come without controversy. Maathai was best known as the founder of the Green Belt Movement (GBM), an initiative to plant trees in forested areas of Kenya that were being stripped for commercial expansion. Critics wondered whether a "tree planter" was truly a peace activist. For Maathai there was an important link between the environment and peace. Most of the people involved with GBM are rural African women who, over the years, have planted nearly thirty million trees. As a result they have reaped the rewards of food, fuel, shelter, and employment. More importantly, they have achieved control over their own lives. In an interview with the *Progressive* Maathai commented on her Nobel win: "I wasn't working on the issue of peace specifically. I was contributing toward peace, and that is what the committee recognized: that, indeed, we need to step back and look at a more expanded concept of peace and security."

Respect for the soil

Wangari Muta Maathai was born on April 1, 1940, in Nyeri, Kenya. The Republic of Kenya is located on the eastern coast of Africa and is divided into seven provinces; Nyeri is the capital of the Central province. Like many Kenyans Maathai came from a

> "We need to rethink our concept of peace and security. We need to look at the way we manage and share our resources. Only then do we have hope."

farming family, and as she remarked to Judith Stone of *O Magazine,* her parents taught her to "respect the soil and its bounty." "I grew up close to my mother," Maathai further explained to Stone, "in the field, where I could observe nature."

Maathai's home life was very much like other Kenyans in other ways as well. Her father was considered the head of the house; her mother had very little power and performed traditional "women's tasks" such as fetching water and gathering firewood. In particular, education for women and girls was not valued, or even encouraged. But Maathai was extremely bright, and her older brother persuaded their parents to send her to school when she was seven years old. She did so well in her studies that in 1960 Maathai earned a scholarship to attend college in the United States.

Maathai attended Mount St. Scholastica College (now Benedictine College) in Atchison, Kansas, where she was known to her classmates as Mary Jo. After earning a bachelor's degree in biology in 1964 she went on to receive a master's degree in biological sciences at the University of Pittsburgh (Pennsylvania) in 1965. In many interviews Maathai claimed that her years in the United States had a profound effect on her, especially since she was exposed to the many demonstrations against the Vietnam War (1954–75; a controversial war in which the United States aided South Vietnam in its fight against a takeover by Communist North Vietnam). Watching Americans express themselves made Maathai realize that people had a right to speak out for what they believed in.

Although she enjoyed her experiences in the United States, Maathai decided to return to Kenya, where, in 1971 she completed her doctoral studies in veterinary anatomy at the University of Nairobi. She was the first woman in East or Central Africa to earn a Ph.D. Maathai then joined the faculty of the university as a professor of veterinary anatomy, becoming the first woman to hold a professorship at the school. During the early 1970s the fledgling instructor married and had three children. Her husband, Mwangi Maathai, was a politician who divorced his wife in the mid-1980s, claiming that she was too educated and too difficult to control.

A simple plan for a complex problem

While still a professor Maathai became involved in politics herself when she joined the National Council of Women of Kenya, an organization devoted to bettering the status of African women. While speaking to people living in rural areas, she discovered that the government had induced farmers to switch from growing crops for themselves to producing cash crops, such as coffee and tea, for exporting. As a result, large expanses of forested land had been cleared to make room for more commercial farm production. Such change had a damaging effect on rural family life, especially for women. They could no longer grow food for their children because nutrients in the soil were depleted; they had no access to firewood, which was their main source of energy;

livestock suffered because there was no vegetation to graze on; and streams were drying up or were polluted by soil runoff, resulting in a lack of drinking water.

Considering how enormous the issues were, Maathai felt that an immediate and straightforward plan was needed. She came up with a simple solution: plant trees. As Maathai explained to Michelle Martin of *Catholic New World,* "It occurred to me that some of the problems women talked about were connected to the land. If you plant trees you give them firewood. If you plant trees you give them food." On Earth Day in 1977 Maathai put her plan into action by planting seven trees to honor Kenyan women environmental leaders. (Earth Day is an annual day set aside to honor and celebrate the environment.) Later that year, with backing from the National Council of Women, the budding environmentalist quit teaching and formed the Green Belt Movement. The group started small, with only a handful of villagers gathering seeds and planting them.

At first, government officials laughed at the program, claiming that only professional foresters knew how to plant trees. But eventually the first small groups of villagers trained other groups and over the next thirty years, more than thirty million trees were planted. Six thousand tree nurseries were created and operated by women, and jobs were provided for more than one hundred thousand people. Most importantly, an enormous power shift occurred as women began to take control of their futures. As authors Anne and Frances Lapp explained in *Mother Earth News,* "Women discovered they were not powerless in the face of oppressive husbands and village chiefs."

Although planting trees was the most visible Green Belt campaign, it was not its only focus. With support from the National Council of Women, Maathai created programs aimed at educating Kenyan women in areas such as family planning, nutrition, and leadership development. The movement also created a food-security campaign to reintroduce crops originally grown in the region and to reestablish kitchen gardens for individual family use.

Green Belt Movement: Women for Change

Since the 2002 elections, the political climate in Kenya took a turn for the better, with government leaders listening more intently to issues affecting women, and in turn allowing women to have more participation in policy decisions. Given this new climate, the Green Belt Movement established a program in 2003 called Women for Change (WFC). Sponsored in part by Comic Relief United Kingdom (a group that provides funding for nonprofit organizations through comedy concerts), the goal of the program is to give women, especially young girls, a new sense of empowerment through education.

In 2003 the president of Kenya, Mwai Kibaki (1931–), declared an official "War on HIV/AIDS" and, in response, WFC instituted training sessions on sexual and reproductive health to teach young women how to protect themselves from becoming infected with the HIV virus and how to avoid early pregnancy. Other WFC initiatives include providing scholarships and tuition assistance to young girls who excel academically, and training women to gain income-generating skills, such as bee keeping.

Now that women are making inroads on the political front in Kenya, WFC hopes to tackle some long-ingrained cultural problems. One way to do that is through the creation of a center for abused women and children. In Kenya women have historically been treated as property by their husbands, and no laws existed to protect women who were mistreated by their spouses. The purpose of the center is to offer safety and shelter to women and children. More importantly it will be an education center for both men and women to break the cycle of abuse.

Powerful political force

As the Green Belt Movement expanded, Maathai found herself increasingly at odds with the Kenyan government. She explained to Amitabh Pal of the *Progressive,* "I started seeing the linkages between the problems that we were dealing with and the root causes.... I knew that a major culprit of environmental destruction was the government." Maathai became an outspoken advocate for environmental policy reform; she also held seminars to educate citizens that they must hold government officials accountable for managing natural resources. One of the first public confrontations came in 1989 when Maathai openly protested the building of a $200 million, sixty-story skyscraper in Nairobi's Uhuru Park that was slated to be used for government offices. Maathai's campaign was so successful that the building was never constructed.

Maathai soon began speaking out against the general corruption that ran wild throughout the administration of then-president Daniel arap Moi (1924–). Moi took office in 1978 and since then had ruled with a strong arm, imprisoning and sometimes torturing anyone suspected of opposing his authority. In 1991 Maathai formalized her political activism by cofounding the Forum for the Restoration of Democracy. As she explained to Michelle Martin, "I started out planting trees and found myself in the forefront of fighting for the restoration of democracy in my country." As a result Maathai became a particular target of Moi's terrorist tactics. For example, in 1992, while participating in a hunger strike with mothers who were protesting the imprisonment of their sons—men who were pro-democracy activists—Maathai was brutally beaten by police.

Throughout the 1990s Maathai was arrested, imprisoned, and intimidated time and again for speaking out against the Moi administration. She remained undaunted, however, and even made several attempts to run for public office. In 1992 Maathai was approached to run for the presidency, but declined. In 1997 she agreed to run both for the presidency under the Liberal Party of Kenya (LPK) and for a seat in the National Assembly. The National Assembly is the ruling body in Kenya (similar to the U. S. Congress) and consists of 210 members who are elected to five-year terms. Prior to the election the LPK withdrew their support of Maathai because of political differences—the party felt she would focus solely on environmental issues. Maathai also lost her bid for a seat in the National Assembly, coming in third.

Because of constitutional restrictions, Moi was now allowed run for another presidential term in the December 2002 elections. Therefore, in the first free and democratic elections held in nearly twenty-five years, Kenyan citizens voted in a new administration, with Mwai Kibaki (1931–) serving as president. During the same elections Maathai won a seat in the National Assembly, taking 98 percent of the vote. According to *Mother Earth News,* "Women danced in the streets of Nairobi for joy." Just a few weeks after Kibaki took over the presidency, he appointed Maathai Deputy Minister of the Environment, Natural Resources and Wildlife.

In 2004 Wangari Maathai was honored with the prestigious Nobel Peace Prize for her lifelong dedication to environmental and human rights. AP/Wide World Photos.

Proponent of peace

Since taking office, Maathai has worked to enact laws to protect not only the environment but also women's rights and human rights. In 2005 she was integral in helping to shape Kenya's new Bill of Rights; she also represented Kenya at the 2005 United Nations Commission on the Status of Women, an international body of representatives convened to promote the rights of women worldwide. In addition, Maathai continued in her role as an internationally recognized environmentalist. By late 2005, through the Pan-African Green Belt Network, over fifteen African countries had become involved with the Green Belt Movement. The movement also spread beyond the African borders to the United States, where representatives work through the Friends of the Greenbelt Movement North America. In 2005 a primary goal of Maathai was to extend the resources of the Green Belt Movement to help other areas of the world, such as the Republic of Haiti, which has also been ravaged by deforestation.

For her lifelong dedication to environmental and human rights Maathai has received numerous awards, including the Goldman Environmental Prize, the Right Livelihood Award, and the United Nation's Africa Prize for Leadership. In 2004 Maathai was honored with the prestigious Nobel Peace Prize, named after Swedish industrialist Alfred Nobel (1833–1896). The award is given annually by the Nobel Committee to individuals or organizations that work to promote peace, resolve conflict, or uphold human rights.

Traditionally, however, past Nobel winners tended to be people who worked for peace during times of war. When Maathai was chosen as the recipient she became the very first environmentalist to be recognized, and many wondered whether a "tree planter" deserved such an honor. Authors Anne and Frances Moore posed the question in *Mother Earth News*: "Why honor environmental activism in an era when war, terrorism and nuclear proliferation are even more urgent problems?" Nobel Committee chair Ole Danbolt Mjos offered a response via a quote in the *Progressive*: "This year, the Norwegian Nobel Committee has evidently broadened its definition of peace still further. Environmental protection has become yet another path to peace."

In her acceptance speech, which was quoted in the *Progressive,* Maathai also acknowledged being the first black woman to be honored with the Nobel: "As the first African woman to receive this prize, I accept it on behalf of the people of Kenya and Africa, and indeed the world." She went on to add, "I am especially mindful of women and the girl child. I hope it will encourage them to raise their voices and take more space for leadership." Following her win Maathai traveled around the world speaking to groups who were charmed by her dazzling smile and classy-but-friendly attitude. According to Judith Stone of *O Magazine* she is a "notoriously terrific hugger." And during Stone's interview with the famous environmentalist, she got a glimpse into Maathai's dedicated personality. "People often ask me what drives me," Maathai revealed. "Perhaps the more difficult question would be: What would it take to stop me?"

For More Information

Books

Maathai, Wangari. *The Green Belt Movement: Sharing the Approach and the Experience*. New York: Lantern Books, 2003.

Periodicals

Lappe, Anna Moore, and Frances Moore Lappe. "The Genius of Wangari Maathai." *Mother Earth News* (April–May 2005): pp. 20–22.

Robinson, Simon. "Wangari Maathai: Why Green Matters." *Time* (April 18, 2005): p. 98.

"Wangari Maathai: First Black Woman to Win the Nobel Peace Prize." *Ebony* (March 2005): p. 22–24.

Web Sites

Friends of the Green Belt Movement North America. http://www.gbmna.org/ (accessed on August 23, 2005).

The Greenbelt Movement. www.greenbeltmovement.org (accessed on August 23, 2005).

Martin, Michelle. "Kenyan Nobel Winner Finds Lessons in Creation." *Catholic New World* (July 17, 2005). http://www.catholicnew world.com/cnw/issue/3_071705.html (accessed on August 23, 2005).

Pal, Amitabh. "Interview with Wangari Maathai." *The Progressive* (May 1, 2005). http://www.gbmna.org/a.php?id = 109 (accessed on August 23, 2005).

Stone, Judith. "Force of Nature." *O Magazine* (May 12, 2005). http://www.gbmna.org/a.php?id = 114 (accessed on August 23, 2005).

Peyton Manning

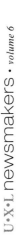

March 24, 1976 • *New Orleans, Louisiana*

Football player

Peyton Manning, starting quarterback for the Indianapolis Colts, may be on his way to becoming America's favorite male sports star. For years that honor was held by basketball legend Michael Jordan (1963–). But a January 2005 Harris poll surveyed American adults and found Peyton Manning nipping at Jordan's heels in the number-two spot. Sports analysts credited Manning's rise in popularity to his amazing performance during the 2004 football season. The six-foot-five quarterback broke several major National Football League (NFL) records, including most touchdown passes in a single season. As a result, Manning was honored with a slew of awards, including the NFL's Most Valuable Player prize for the second year in a row. In addition to being lauded for his abilities on the gridiron, Manning received numerous awards for his generous giving spirit. In April 2005 he was presented with the Byron "Whizzer" White Award, which, according to its official Web site, is given annually to the NFL player who "best personifies the spirit of service to team, community and country.

Football family

Peyton Manning was born on March 24, 1976, in New Orleans, Louisiana, the middle son of Archie (1949–) and Olivia Peyton. Peyton's father, Archie, was a celebrated football star, playing quarterback in college for the University of Mississippi and for

> "I think that's why I have a love for football still today, because it was fun for me as a kid."

various NFL teams during the 1970s and early 1980s, including the New Orleans Saints and the Minnesota Vikings. The elder Peyton went on to become a radio sports announcer for the Saints. When they were young, Manning and his brothers, Eli (1981–) and Cooper (c. 1974–), enjoyed tagging along with their father when the Saints were in town practicing during the off season. Sometimes the players and renowned coach Jim Mora (1935–) would even let the boys toss the ball around on the field.

While attending Isidore Newman High School in New Orleans, Peyton participated in a variety of sports. He was on the basketball team for two years and played shortstop on the baseball team. But football was his true passion—a passion he credits his father for instilling in him. Manning, however, is quick to note in interviews that Archie never pushed him into the sport. As he explained on his official Web site, "It was a policy in the house growing up, [Dad] would help us out and be glad to play catch with us ... but we had to go to him for help. He wasn't going to come to us and say, 'All right, you do this, you do that.'"

Manning honed his skills by practicing with his brothers and neighborhood friends. He also spent hours listening to and studying tapes of his father's old college and professional football games. By the time he was a sophomore at Isidore Newman, Manning was talented enough to be the starting quarterback; that same year his older brother, Cooper, was the team's wide receiver. The Manning boys became an inseparable pair both on the field and off, and worked so well together that the duo took their team all the way to the state Class 2A semifinals. Following his senior year Cooper accepted a scholarship to attend the college where his father played—the University of Mississippi, also known as Ole Miss. Unfortunately, during Cooper's freshman year, doctors discovered a spinal weakness, which caused a numbness in his legs and forced him to abandon his football career.

Victory for Volunteers

During his years at Isidore Newman, Manning was the undisputed star of the team and ended up with impressive statistics: He passed for 7,207 yards and completed 59.4 percent of his passes with 92 touchdowns. As a senior he was named the Gatorade National High School Player of the Year and was being scouted by all the top colleges in the United States. A great deal of pressure was put on him by Ole Miss fans and alumni to attend the University of Mississippi, but after much consideration the quarterback decided to head to the University of Tennessee in Knoxville to play for the Tennessee Volunteers. As he explained in interviews, he wanted a challenge. At Ole Miss he was already a celebrity before having played a single game. At the University of Tennessee, he would have to prove himself.

Before heading to Knoxville, the ever diligent Manning prepared himself by poring over footage of Volunteer games and studying the team's playbook. During the first part of his freshman year Manning sat on the bench, but he quickly got a chance to share the starting quarterback duties with fellow freshman Brandon Stewart after two of the team's top players were sidelined by injuries. As a starter Manning led the Volunteers to victory in six of the next seven games, which qualified them to play in the Gator Bowl. (The Gator Bowl is an annual competition played between two of the top college football teams; other bowl games include the Rose Bowl and Orange Bowl as well as several others.)

The Volunteers trounced Virginia Tech in a 45–23 win, and Manning, having thrown for 1,141 yards, 11 touchdowns, and 6 interceptions, cemented himself as a core player.

Stewart transferred to Texas A&M University before the beginning of the 1995 season, which left Manning as the sole starting quarterback. With Manning at the helm, the Volunteers made it to the Citrus Bowl in 1995 and 1996 (winning both years), and the Orange Bowl in 1997, where they were defeated by the Nebraska Cornhuskers. Manning rounded out his senior year by leading his team to the Eastern Division Southeastern Conference (SEC) championship in 1997. Colleges that belong to the National Collegiate Athletic Association (NCAA) are divided into three divisions: Division I-A; Division I-AA; and Division II. Within each division colleges are organized by geographic location; the University of Tennessee is part of the Eastern Division of the Southeastern Conference.

During his four-year Tennessee tenure the star quarterback amassed an impressive array of records. He established thirty-three passing records, becoming the university's all-time leading passer with 11,201 yards, 863 completions, and 89 touchdowns. Manning's accurate throwing arm also helped him set several SEC records in passing yards, pass completions, and completion percentage. In addition, many believed he would be a shoe-in to win the Heisman Trophy, which is awarded annually to the best college football player in the United States. Manning lost to cornerback Charles Woodson (1976–) of the University of Michigan, but he took home both the Davey O'Brien and Johnny Unitas awards, which honor the best college quarterbacks in the nation. In early 1998 Manning also nabbed the Sullivan Award, an annual prize given to the best amateur athlete in the United States.

Peyton the pro

At the University of Tennessee Manning was a communications and business major, and he completed his bachelor's degree requirements in just three years, ending up with a 3.6 grade point average. As a result, he was eligible to graduate at the end of his junior year. The NFL was knocking at his door, but Manning decided to hold off going pro until after his senior year. As he explained on his official Web site, "My college experience was a really good one, so I decided to stay all four years. I just wanted to enjoy being a college senior. For some reason people had a very hard time believing that." The wait paid off, and in 1998 a very mature and poised Manning became the NFL number-one draft pick and was snatched up by the Indianapolis Colts. The coach for the Colts just happened to be old family friend Jim Mora, who had watched a very young Manning toss the ball around back in New Orleans.

The pressure was on Manning his rookie year because the Colts had traded former starting quarterback Jim Harbaugh (1963–) to make room for him on the roster. The team had also paid Manning a top dollar contract: $48 million over six years. The fresh-faced Manning started off slow, but quickly brought his game up to professional speed through perseverance, practice, and his standby method of studying football film footage late into the night before every game. He remarked to Michael Silver of *Sports Illustrated,* "I've never left the field saying, 'I could have done more to get ready,' and that gives me peace of mind." Over the next few years the starting quarterback also earned the respect and admiration of his fellow players and coaches, both for his easygoing demeanor and his fierce competitiveness. As Colts' coach Tony Dungy (1955–) told Silver, "I've never seen a guy with so much ability and the dedication to match."

Manning's dedication repeatedly paid off for the Colts. Although the team ended the 1998 season with a 3 win, 13 loss record, over the next few years the signal-calling Manning led Indianapolis to the American Football Conference (AFC) division championships five times. The thirty-two football teams that are part of the NFL are divided evenly into two conferences: the AFC and the National Football Conference (NFC). Within each conference, there are four divisions: North, South, East, and West. Out of the five championship games, the Colts took the AFC title three times: in 1999, 2003, and 2004.

By 2005, Manning was also a champion in his own right, having played, according to Michael Silver, "The best football of

Peyton Manning made football history on December 26, 2004, when he broke the record for most touchdown passes in a single season. © Tim Johnson/ Reuters/Corbis.

his career." In a particularly anticipated achievement, Manning made football history on December 26, 2004, when he broke the record for most touchdown passes in a single season. By completing his forty-ninth pass Manning broke the record of forty-eight previously held by Dan Marino (1961–) of Miami Dolphins fame. The on-fire quarterback also set several other NFL records, including becoming the only player to pass for more than four thousand yards in six consecutive seasons; the only player to score four touchdowns or more in five consecutive games; and the only quarterback to start in every single game of his NFL career.

Peyton pays back

According to his brother, Cooper, who spoke with John Bradley of *Sports Illustrated,* "Peyton's got the potential to be one of the greatest quarterbacks of all time." Whether or not that is true is yet to be seen. The Colts, however, believed in him: In March 2004 they signed Manning to a $99.2 million, seven-year contract, which included an NFL-record $34.5 million signing bonus. Members of the Associated Press also believed in Manning, naming him the NFL's Most Valuable Player in both 2003 and 2004. Manning is only the third player in history to receive the award two years in a row. In addition, in 2005 the Colts' quarterback took home a number of other top honors, including *The Sporting News* Player of the Year Award and an ESPY for Best NFL Player. (ESPY awards are awarded to America's top athletes each year by the sports network ESPN.)

For Manning, however, the highest honor may have come in April 2005 when he was given the prestigious Byron "Whizzer" White Humanitarian Award, named for Supreme Court Justice and former NFL player Byron White (1917–2002). Established in 1967 by the professional football players of America, the prize acknowledges White's spirit of giving back to the community. "I am truly humbled by this honor," Manning remarked in a press release issued on July 20, 2005, "This means a lot to me because what I do off the field is much more important than anything I do on the field."

Manning's accomplishments off the field were truly impressive. In 1999 he created the PeyBack Foundation, the goal of which, according to Manning's Web site, "is to provide leadership and growth opportunities for children at risk." As of 2005 the foundation has donated over $900,000 to children's programs in Indiana, Tennessee, and Louisiana. The big-hearted Manning participates personally in the majority of the foundation's initiatives, including Peyton's Pals, which sponsors a series of monthly cultural and educational events for selected Indianapolis middle-schoolers. One of the most high-profile events is the PeyBack Classic, an annual event in which Indiana inner-city high school football players are invited to play ball at the Indianapolis RCA Dome. All proceeds benefit struggling high school sports programs.

Manning Award Winner: Matt Leinart

In 2004 the Sugar Bowl Committee established the Manning Award, the newest award in the National Collegiate Athletic Association (NCAA) to honor top college quarterbacks. The award was named in honor of three NFL players all from the same family: father Archie Manning (1949–), a former NFL quarterback during the 1970s and early 1980s, and sons Peyton (1976–), quarterback for the Indianapolis Colts, and Eli (1981–), quarterback for the New York Giants. The prize will be awarded each year following completion of all bowl games. In 2005, the first recipient of the Manning Award was University of Southern California (USC) quarterback Matt Leinart.

Leinart was born May 11, 1983, in Santa Ana, California. Like Peyton Manning, he distinguished himself early on in football while playing for Mater Dei Catholic High School, where, during his senior year he earned numerous honors, including being named the Gatorade California Player of the Year. Throughout his freshman and sophomore years at USC Leinart was a third-string quarterback and saw little action, but by the end of spring training 2003 he had edged his way into the starting quarterback position. The left-handed passer began as a little-known player, but by the end of his junior year he was one of the most acclaimed quarterbacks in USC history. He established several school passing records and in 2004 snagged a slew of national awards, including the Heisman Trophy, considered by many the most prestigious honor in college football.

Leinart, like Manning, decided to finish college rather than turn professional early. As he explained to Austin Murphy of *Sports Illustrated,* "My decision was seen as something good for college football, a statement to kids to stay in school." Since winning the Heisman, the six-foot-five Leinart traveled around the United States to offer his own unique brand of inspiration. He freely talked about overcoming the medical condition he was born with called strabismus, which means he was born cross-eyed. Leinart had two surgeries to correct the problem: one when he was a little over one year old, the other as a high school freshman. He told Murphy, "I talk about how battling obstacles as a young kid will make you a stronger person."

In an interview with *Sports Illustrated,* Peyton commented, "I would like to leave some kind of unique mark on the game." Given his astonishing number of passing records, his amazing number of awards, and his generosity off the field, the young man who was born into football royalty and who, in 2005, was at the height of his career, already seemed to have left his mark.

For More Information

Periodicals

Attner, Paul. "Blessed and Obsessed: No One Wants to Translate Regular-season Greatness into Postseason Success More than

Peyton Manning and the Colts." *The Sporting News* (January 14, 2005): p. 20–25.

Bradley, John. "Cooper on Peyton." *Sports Illustrated* (November 10, 2003): p. 84.

Murphy, Austin. "Matt Leinart: USC Quarterback." *Sports Illustrated* (July 25, 2005): p. 35.

Sabino, David. "Season to Remember."*Sports Illustrated* (December 20, 2004): p. 52.

Silver, Michael. "Hand Him the MVP." *Sports Illustrated* (December 22, 2003): p. 40.

Silver, Michael. "Passing Marks: The Colts' Peyton Manning." *Sports Illustrated* (December 20, 2004): p. 48.

Web Sites

Banks, Don. "Peyton Manning Headlines List of Year-End Award Recipients." *SI.com: Banks' Shots* (January 3, 2005). http://sports illustrated.cnn.com/2005/writers/don_banks/01/03/banks.yearend/index.html (accessed on August 23, 2005).

Peyton Manning Official Web Site. http://www.peytonmanning.com/ (accessed on August 23, 2005).

Silver, Michael. "A Sense of History: If Anyone Appreciates His Place Amongst Elite QBs, It's Peyton Manning." *SI.com: Open Mike* (December 17, 2004). http://sportsillustrated.cnn.com/2004/writers/michael_silver/12/17/silver.manning/index.html (accessed on August 23, 2005).

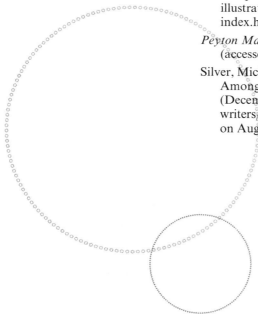

Maroon 5

Rock band

According to the press, and summed up by Walter Tunis of the *Lexington Herald-Leader,* Maroon 5 was "one of the hottest new pop rock bands in the land." In February 2005 the music industry added its approval to the statement by presenting Maroon 5 with a Grammy Award for Best New Artist. Ironically, although considered new on the music scene, the band actually had been performing together for ten years. In addition, their success in 2005 was built around an album, *Songs about Jane,* that was three years old. Since the album's 2002 release Maroon 5 toured almost nonstop, and thanks to word of mouth, their fan base slowly grew. As a result several singles, including "This Love" and "She Will Be Loved," began receiving constant airplay on radio and MTV, and finally settled comfortably at the top of the U.S. song charts.

Kara's Flowers

Maroon 5 is composed of five members: lead singer Adam Levine (March 18, 1979); keyboardist Jesse Carmichael; bass player

Mickey Madden; lead guitarist James Valentine (October 5, 1978); and drummer Ryan Dusick. Except for Valentine, who was born in Lincoln, Nebraska, the band members all hail from Los Angeles, California. Dusick and Levine had known each other since they were kids and in high school they joined forces with Madden and Carmichael to form an alternative-rock band called Kara's Flowers.

"We were really young," Levine commented to Larry Katz of the *Boston Herald.* "We were into Green Day, Weezer, and Beatles-inspired weirdness." In 1995, the foursome played their first official gig at the famous Los Angeles club the

---

"I don't think we ever thought we would be this big. It's very humbling."

Adam Levine

Whiskey-a-Go-Go. Shortly afterward they signed a record deal with the Warner Brothers' label Reprise Records. Such early success left little time for academics. As Levine explained to Katz, "We went to this prep school called Brentwood, where I was doing really badly because I was spending my time writing music instead of doing homework. . . . I miraculously graduated because I could say, 'Sorry, I didn't do that paper because I was in the studio'."

Although they did not excel academically at Brentwood, the boys did become quite the school stars, picking up a loyal following in and around L.A. As Kara's Flowers they released their first and only album, called *The Fourth World,* in mid-1997. Levine, Carmichael, and Madden were seniors in high school, and Dusick, who is slightly older, was a sophomore at the University of California, Los Angeles. They toured briefly and shot one video for MTV for the single "Soap Disco." The album, however, never really took off. In 1999 Reprise Records released them from their contract, and Kara's Flowers disbanded.

Maroon 5 pose with their awards for Best New Artist at the Grammy Awards. From left: Mickey Madden, James Valentine, Adam Levine, Ryan Dusick, and Jesse Carmichael. AP/Wide World Photos.

Band turns maroon

The foursome separated when Madden decided to attend UCLA with Dusick, and Levine and Carmichael headed to New York to attend Five Towns College, a small liberal arts school on Long Island. The experience was a major turning point for the transplanted Californians. As Levine explained to David Hiltbrand of the *Philadelphia Inquirer,* "We had never lived anywhere but L.A. It was a different world, a really cool experience." Living in the dorms introduced Levine and Carmichael to a variety of music styles, from hip-hop to gospel music to rhythm and blues—styles that would eventually influence their future sound. Levine was inspired by one artist in particular. "My singing style changed so much," he told Hiltbrand. "All I knew when I was younger was Paul McCartney and Paul Simon. Listening to Stevie Wonder changed everything."

Less than two years into their college experience, Levine and Carmichael returned to L.A. with renewed energy. They called their friends Dusick and Madden and began playing as a band again. Carmichael, however, had switched from guitar to playing keyboards, so a fifth member, James Valentine (formerly of the band Square), was brought on board in 2001 to round out the group. With a fresh sound and a new band mate, the group decided to change their name first to Maroon, eventually settling on Maroon 5. The reason for the name remains a bit of a mystery: According to some, it was inspired by a fictional band called Yellow 5, which is featured on the Web-based comic *Pokey the Penguin.*

Levine and Valentine became Maroon 5's primary songwriters, and with new songs in hand the band began playing gigs in New York and Los Angeles. They were soon signed by a small New York label called Octone Records, which is part of J Records and BMG, one of the largest companies in the music industry. In 2002 the band entered the studio and recorded their first album as Maroon 5. Called *Songs about Jane,* the majority of the tracks were written by Levine, who had just gone through a difficult break up with his girlfriend.

Funk-soul-pop-rock

Even before the album was released in June 2002, Maroon 5's record company booked the band on a constant touring schedule, which meant opening for a number of established performers, including Matchbox Twenty, Sheryl Crow (1963–), and John Mayer (1977–). At the same time, the album's first single, "Harder to Breathe," was slowly climbing up the charts thanks to a loyal fan base built by nonstop touring. (By mid-2003 Maroon 5 had performed more than two hundred live shows across the United States.) In October 2003, after sixteen months on the music charts, "Harder to Breathe" finally broke into the top twenty on Billboard's Hot 100. According to Levine, who spoke with Edna Gundersen of *USA Today,* the song caught on for three reasons: "It's a very radio-friendly track, the band does great live shows, and we're not bad-looking either."

Because Maroon 5 was on the road so often, critics had ample opportunity to review their shows. The responses were mixed. Some critics, like Jon Pareles of the *New York Times*, commented on the band's craftsmanship, comparing Levine's vocals to Michael Jackson's (1958–) and their guitar rhythms to the 1980s band The Police, whose lead singer was Sting (1951–). Others were less kind. For example, Darryl Morden of the *Hollywood Reporter* called the band's music bland and tame, and went on to write, "Maroon 5 may understand the blueprints to create the machinery, but the results are shrill, clunky and obvious."

Two things, however, remained constant in the majority of reviews. First, critics had a difficult time categorizing the band. Since Maroon 5 borrowed from so many different types of music, most writers used multi-hyphenated terms in their descriptions. For example, Larry Katz of the *Boston Herald* called them a "funk-soul-pop-rock" outfit. Members of the band were delighted that they did not fit neatly into one category. As Levine told Katz, "It's so much more fun to come in and have people not know what it is you're doing."

The other observation that ran through reviews was that lead singer Adam Levine, with his dark good looks, seemed to be the undisputed leader of the group. In many interviews he served as Maroon 5's spokesman, and it was Levine who ruled the spotlight during performances. According to Christopher Blagg of the *Boston Herald,* "Levine stalks the stage with a cocky strut, preening for the adoring coeds in the front row."

Best new artist

Impressed by the band's growing popularity, J Records launched an all-out promotional campaign for *Songs about Jane*. Maroon 5 went back out on the road, but this time they headlined their own tour. Two more singles were also released: the bouncy pop tune "This Love" and the softer ballad "She Will Be Loved." Videos were shot for the two songs, and both became staples on MTV throughout 2003 and 2004.

By the end of 2004, although they loved performing live, the members of Maroon 5 were starting to become weary.

Maroon 5's Adam Levine, right, and James Valentine during the band's performance at Live 8, the series of global concerts dedicated to erasing poverty in Africa. Timothy A. Clary/AFP/Getty Images.

After all, they had been on the road for almost three years. They used part of the time to write songs for a new album, but the success of their debut CD refused to die down. "This Love" and "She Will Be Loved" climbed to number 5 on the U.S. music charts and reached even higher spots on music charts in other countries. For example, the CD peaked at number one in both the United Kingdom and Australia. And new fans continued to discover the band as more singles, such as "Sunday Morning," were released.

On February 6, 2004, Maroon 5 celebrated their ten-year anniversary; that same day *Songs about Jane* went platinum, meaning at least one million copies were sold in the United States. A year later, in 2005, the CD reached triple-platinum sales, and it was still climbing the charts even though it had debuted more than three years earlier. In February 2005, however, the quintet received their biggest payoff when they were nominated for two Grammy Awards: Pop Performance by a Duo or Group with Vocal for "She Will Be Loved" and Best New Artist. Grammy Awards are given annually to honor the top recording artists in over 105 music categories.

Producer and rapper **Kanye West** (1977–; see entry) was the favorite to win the Best New Artist award, but in a surprising twist the prize went to Maroon 5. "It was genuinely shocking," Levine told Larry Katz. "I really didn't think it was going to happen." John Soeder of the *Plain Dealer* called the award "the cherry on a sweet victory sundae nearly three years in the making."

Grittier future

Winning a Grammy may have been sweet victory, but members of Maroon 5 were not ready to rest yet. In mid-2005 Levine and Valentine were hard at work putting the finishing touches on songs for their sophomore album, slated to be released in 2006. And, of course, they were still touring, this time opening for the Rolling Stones on their 2005 North American tour. The band continued playing favorites from *Songs about Jane,* but they were also trying out new material for fans—material with a harder, more gritty sound.

In interviews the band mates did not seem worried about turning off fans who were used to their more soft-rock sound. "We started off with a clean slate," Levine explained to Larry Katz, "and we can only dirty it up on the next record. We're ready to do that. We're ready to change things a bit so people won't have the same perceptions of us. It will definitely be different, I can tell you that." In addition, after ten years of playing together the band seemed unconcerned about reviewers who, according to Katz, dismissed them as a "lightweight band of L.A. pretty boys." "We ARE lightweight L.A. pretty boys," Levine laughingly responded, "We're skinny dudes, we're attractive, we make pop music. It's a no-brainer. We're the easiest targets imaginable."

For More Information

Periodicals

Blagg, Christopher. "Maroon 5 Looking a Little Green." *Boston Herald* (April 4, 2005): p. 040.

Gunderson, Edna. "Slow-building Single Keeps Maroon 5's Star Rising." *USA Today* (October 13, 2003): p. 01D.

Hiltbrand, David. "Marooned on the Road: Singer-Strummer Talks About Life with Eclectic Band." *Philadelphia Inquirer* (October 30, 2003).

Katz, Larry. "Maroon Shot: Best New Band Heads for New Arena." *Boston Herald* (April 1, 2005).

Katz, Larry. "Stranded Maroon 5 Finally Breaks Through the 'Harder' Way." *Boston Herald* (October 29, 2003): p. 052.

Laban, Linda. "Maroon 5 Singer Wants to Go Out on Top." *Boston Herald* (August 19, 2004): p. 061.

Macdonald, Patrick. "These Are Red-Letter Days for Colorful Maroon 5." *Seattle Times* (April 29, 2005): p. 14.

Morden, Darryl. "Maroon 5: Concert Review." *Hollywood Reporter* (September 30, 2003): p. 20.

Pareles, Jon. "Macho Rock on the Surface, with Wimpiness Underneath." *New York Times* (April 8, 2005): p. E4L.

Soeder, John. "Maroon 5 Singer Levine Says Group Plans 'Amazing' Album." *The Plain Dealer (Cleveland, Ohio)* (April 15, 2005): p. 6.

Tunis, Walter. "Maroon 5 Band Mates Break Through on Second Shot at Fame." *Lexington Herald-Leader* (October 23, 2003).

Web Sites

Maroon 5 Web Site. http://www.maroon5.com/main_site/main.html (accessed on July 27, 2005).

Jenny Ming

1955 • *Canton, China*

Chief executive officer

Jenny Ming is president of Old Navy, the enormously successful chain of clothing stores owned by Gap, Inc. A retail executive her entire career, Ming has won praise for her skilled management of the 850-store Old Navy division and the seemingly effortless way new fashion trends appear on its racks. She has been with Old Navy since its start in 1994, as part of the team of Gap executives chosen to help launch it, and she was promoted to president in 1999. In 2004, thanks to her impressive track record overseeing a division whose sales had actually outpaced those of its parent company, Ming made her second appearance on *Fortune* magazine's list of the "50 Most Powerful Women in American Business."

Family walks to freedom

Ming was born in Canton, China, in 1955. Six years earlier, a Communist revolution led by Mao Zedong (1893–1976) had come to power in China, and many middle-class Chinese or those opposed to one-party rule were harassed. (Communism is a system of government in which the state plans and controls the economy and a single party holds power.) The government also confiscated property, and in some cases professionals were forced to take menial labor jobs as part of a "re-education" campaign, which was designed to remake the middle classes into fully supportive communists. When Ming was three months old, her parents decided to flee the country and go to Macao, a small peninsula and two-island territory located on the coast of China's Guangdong Province. At the time, Macao was a

> "[Jenny] Ming has shown an uncanny knack for predicting which hip-looking clothes of the moment will appeal to the masses, then making big bets on producing the huge quantities needed to assure the chain a continual string of hits."
>
> *Business Week*

Portuguese colony, and had been since the late sixteenth century. Like nearby Hong Kong, a colony belonging to Great Britain, Macao did not become part of Communist China until many years later.

Ming's family had to walk most of the way to Macao. Her parents carried her, while her four-year-old sister and two-year-old brother hiked alongside on the half-day trip. They stayed in Macao for several years until Ming's father, who was a printer by trade, took them to America around 1964, when she was nine years old. No longer the baby of the family, she was the middle child of five by then, and they settled in the North Beach neighborhood of San Francisco. Ming recalled her first years as an immigrant quite clearly, even forty years later. "I wanted to be

American so badly," she told *New York Times* journalist Amy Zipkin. "I loved the food. I loved Halloween: I couldn't believe there was a holiday where they gave out candy. I didn't have a costume, only a mask. Early in the evening I tripped, fell and cut my chin. The blood dripped down my neck. No one noticed."

Ming was an ambitious teen and eager to earn her own income. She worked as a bank teller and as a salesperson at Macy's department store when she was a high school student. Like many teenage girls of the era, she also sewed her own clothes. She became so skilled at it that she took out a newspaper ad offering her seamstress services. She was deeply interested in fashion, but her mother hoped she would become a pharmacist, a profession of some prestige. Instead she studied home economics at San Jose State University. Ming's nineteen-year-old daughter, Kameron, interviewed her for an article that appeared in a 2005 issue of *CosmoGIRL!* and Ming explained how she discovered her career path. Ming recalled that her college-era boyfriend at the time—Kameron's future father—pointed out to her one day, "'You love clothes; you should be a retail buyer. You should take some business classes.'" Ming said. "I thought, Why not? Thinking back, that was a really big turning point."

Boss calls her a "pushover"

Ming graduated from San Jose State in 1978 with a bachelor of arts in clothing merchandising, with a minor in marketing. Her first job was at a Mervyn's department store in Colma, California, as an assistant manager in the hosiery department. She was transferred to the store's linens department as a manager and recalled that the saleswomen she was supervising there were older, part-time employees, mostly homemakers who took the job as a way to get out of the house. They treated Ming like a daughter, and she had some trouble asserting her authority at first. Aside from ringing up sales, not a lot of work seemed to get done in linens. "They'd just talk or take breaks," Ming told her daughter in the *CosmoGIRL!* interview. The store manager soon noticed the problem, and called Ming into the office to tell her, "'You're never going to make it in this business because you're such a pushover,'" Ming recalled.

"I was heartbroken," Ming remembered feeling that day. "I'd only been in the business nine months and already someone was saying I wasn't going to make it! That night I talked to your dad and he said, 'Just tell them what you need from them.'" She went back to work the next day and assembled her staff, telling them, 'I need you to do what you signed on to do. If not, you'll get a new manager who is not going to be as nice as I am.'" The women liked Ming and wanted her to succeed in her first job. Their work habits improved, and soon the junior linens-department boss was earning high marks for her management skills.

Ming moved over to junior wear at Mervyn's before she was personally recruited by Gap's chief executive officer, Millard S. Drexler (1944–), in 1986. She joined the San Francisco-based retailer that year as a buyer for its activewear division, and rose quickly within Gap management ranks thanks to her ability to forecast what would sell. For example, she thought that customers might like to see Gap's affordable T-shirts in the stores all the year round, not just in the spring/summer months, and she also expanded the basic T-shirt line from six shades to dozens of hot fashion colors.

Enlists in Old Navy

Ming became a Gap vice president after three years on the job. In 1994, Drexler named her as a member of a new executive team that would oversee a planned Gap spin-off, to be called Old Navy. The Old Navy stores would sell affordable casualwear basics for men, women, and children. The first Old Navy opened its doors in 1994 in Colma, California, not far from the first job Ming had out of college at Mervyn's. She initially served as senior vice president of merchandising for Old Navy, with responsibilities for production, planning, and distribution. In 1996, she became executive vice president of merchandising for the chain and helped fine-tune the funky, retro-Americana look, with amusing vintage fixtures and signs, for which its stores had become known. She was named president in March 1999.

Old Navy had grown impressively in the five years since that first store had opened in Colma. It reached the $1-billion

A History of Gap

- 1969: Don Fisher opens the first Gap store on San Francisco's Ocean Avenue, near the campus of San Francisco State University, with his wife Doris. Don Fisher's business experience was in hotels and real estate, but when blue jeans began to become popular in the late 1960s, he had a hard time finding ones that fit his six-foot, one-inch frame properly. He contracted with Levi Strauss & Co., the San Francisco-based jeans maker, to supply the first Gap store with jeans in dozens of variations on waist measurement and length. The company's name came from an often-debated topic of the day, the growing "generation gap" between young people who seemed more relaxed and outrageous and their parents who seemed more reserved and conservative.

- 1970: Gap's second store opens in San Jose, California; sales reach $2 million.

- 1974: Gap kicks off a new "Fall into Gap" advertising campaign; stores also introduce the first private-label Gap merchandise.

- 1976: Gap, Inc. becomes a publicly traded company with an initial public offering (IPO) of stock, with its shares listed on the New York and Pacific Stock exchanges.

- 1983: Gap buys Banana Republic, a two-store company that sold safari and travel gear.

- 1986: The first GapKids store opens in Hillsdale, California.

- 1987: The first overseas Gap store opens on George Street in London, England.

- 1992: Gap becomes the second-largest selling apparel brand in the world.

- 1994: Gap opens its first Old Navy store in Colma, California.

- 1996: Japan gets its first Gap store in a Tokyo retail district.

- 1997: Gap.com, the company's online store, is launched on the Internet.

- 2003: Don Fisher announces his retirement as board chair of Gap, Inc., and is succeeded the following year by his son, Bob.

- 2004: Company revenues reach $16.3 billion. The store is the largest specialty retailer in the United States.

sales mark in 1997, which retail analysts claimed made it the fastest-growing apparel retail start-up in American business history. By 1999, the year that Ming became president, sales figures from Old Navy stores—513 in all by then—were higher than those from Gap stores. Recognizing a successful concept, Gap executives okayed a major expansion of Old Navy, with a hundred new stores set to open each year. Old Navy had caught on with shoppers because of its reasonable prices for items like cargo pants, one of the trends that Ming forecast early on. "One thing

I know best is when to maximize something," she told *Business Week*. "If I believe in something, I'll push it bigger and harder."

By 2002, there were 842 Old Navy stores across the United States, but further expansion plans were halted after the downturn in the American economy that began in 2001. Though Old Navy had done extremely well under Ming, retail analysts believed that because some of its merchandise was similar to—but cheaper than—lines Gap carried in its stores, this had ultimately threatened the health of the parent company. Gap, Inc.'s overall sales, profit, and stock performance had suffered. Drexler retired in 2002 after nineteen years with the company and was replaced by a Disney executive. Ming's new boss was Paul Pressler (1956–), who had formerly run Walt Disney Theme Parks and Resorts. Recognizing Ming's talents, Gap's board of directors made no changes to the Old Navy executive team.

In 2004, Old Navy celebrated its tenth anniversary in business with a new series of the amusing television ads for which the company had become known. Several celebrities had appeared in the winning ad campaigns over the years, including the late *New York Times* fashion writer Carrie Donovan (1928–2001) and television-soap vixen Morgan Fairchild (1950–). The 2004 tenth-anniversary campaign featured former *Dynasty* star Joan Collins (1933–) along with Sherman Helmsley (1938–) and Isabelle Sanford (1917–2004), who played husband and wife on the popular 1970s-era sitcom *The Jeffersons*. Sales from Old Navy stores continued to exceed those from Gap. Old Navy posted $6.7 billion in sales in 2004, while Gap's U.S. stores moved $5.7 billion in merchandise.

Consults with her own kids

Under Ming, Old Navy continued to introduce fresh, fashion-forward items at affordable prices. Ming devoted a large part of her work life to spotting new trends, and some of her off-work time as well. She was visiting London once and noticed that teens were wearing blue jeans with a darker shade of denim. "So I thought, 'Let's darken our stonewash a little,'" she told *Business Week* in 2000. "Now, we have a whole section of dark denim." Ming was also known to interrogate her three teenaged children about trends that were either coming or going. Once, she dropped one of the two daughters off at school on a planned "Pajama Day" and noticed that the teen girls were wearing what her daughter had chosen to wear, too—men's pajama bottoms, belted, with a tank top. "I drove away wondering, Why do we have PJ tops? They never wear them," she recalled in an interview with *Fast Company*. "At the same time, we couldn't sell a lot of pajama sets." Ming voiced the idea of selling just pajama bottoms, and the line became a best-seller at Old Navy stores.

Ming's hobbies include cooking and tennis. Her husband, Mitchell, is involved in the Sonoma County, California, winery industry. When asked by James J. Owens, a writer for a publication of the University of Southern California's Marshall School of Business, what she considered her greatest accomplishment, Ming replied that it was the fact that she had managed to have both a career and a family. "You don't have to sacrifice your personal life for a career," she told Owens. "I never stopped working to have a family. I took six weeks off and came back to work." Some of the thanks for being able to achieve that balance came from the Gap corporate atmosphere itself; among its fifty-one corporate officers, a record twenty-one are women.

Owens also asked her what kind of legacy she hoped to leave behind. She said she hoped it would be "the team of people who take over. I want the business to thrive and I want whoever replaces me to take the business to another level. I also want to leave behind the process of democratizing our brand: students who make very little money shop in our stores, but so do people who can afford to pay more."

For More Information

Periodicals

Caminiti, Susan. "Will Old Navy Fill the Gap?" *Fortune* (March 18, 1996): p. 59.

"Fast Talk: Better by Design." *Fast Company* (June 2004).

Ming, Kameron. "Shop to the Top!" *CosmoGIRL!* (March 2005): p. 118.

Nothum, T.R. "Top Woman." *Future* (Winter 2005).

"Old Navy's Skipper." *Business Week* (January 10, 2000): p. 64.

"A Savvy Captain for Old Navy." *Business Week* (November 8, 1999): p. 130.

"Why Gap Isn't Galloping Anymore." *Business Week* (November 8, 1999): p. 136.

Zipkin, Amy, and Jenny J. Ming. "Tying the Two Strands." *New York Times* (October 27, 2002): p. BU14.

Web Sites

Executive Leadership Team Biographies: Jenny Ming. http://www.gapinc.com/public/About/abt_leader_ming.shtml (accessed on August 23, 2005).

Women in Leadership Conference: Keynote. http://www.wilconference.org/2003/keynote.html (accessed on August 23, 2005).

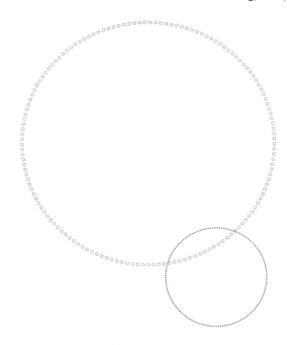

Dave Mirra

AP/Wide World Photos.

April 4, 1974 • *Chittenango, New York*

Extreme sports athlete

Dave Mirra has won more medals in the X Games (a yearly competition held for extreme sports athletes) than any other athlete. What began as a way to pass time became the BMX biker's road to fame and wealth when Mirra turned pro at seventeen. In 1993 he was sidelined for six months after being hit by a drunk driver. The accident nearly killed him, but Mirra came back to win several X Games gold medals in the late 1990s. In 2005 Mirra won his record eighteenth X Games medal and won the ESPY Award for Best Male Action Sports Athlete of 2005.

BMX becomes a sport

David Michael Mirra was born on April 4, 1974, in the small New York town of Chittenango. His parents divorced when he was just five years old, and Dave and his brother,

Tim, were raised by their dad. His mother, Linda, lived nearby in Syracuse and spent time with her sons on a regular basis.

As is typical of boys their age, Dave and Tim spent most of their free time riding their bikes around the neighborhood with their buddies. Small towns don't offer much else to do, and in the early 1980s, Mirra and his brother noticed a few of the other kids in town were riding BMX. (Although BMX stands for "bicycle motorcross," it also has meaning as a term used to describe a sport that includes racing on hilly or sandy tracks as well as on flat land using ramps and obstacles. Bikers use their

> "Anything you want to get better at is a commitment. Without commitment, there would be no success."

20-inch bikes to perform tricks and stunts throughout the race.) They used whatever they could find for jumps. Mirra and his friends were hooked. They began using wooden ramps, curbs, and dirt blocks as jumps. It was then that he began inventing his own gravity-defying stunts that eventually earned him the nickname "Miracle Boy."

Within a couple years, freestyle BMX had gained in popularity. It was no longer a spectacle to see kids performing stunts and tricks on their bikes. Around the age of thirteen, Mirra got noticed for his flatland racing ability (no jumps). It was around this time he realized he might actually be able to turn his hobby into something more. He and his friends already spent nearly every waking moment of the summer—and most of their free time during the school year—on their bikes, challenging and encouraging one another. Mirra's level of dedication to the sport had always been more intense than that of his pals, a key factor in determining how far he would one day take his abilities.

One thing leads to another

Mirra attended a General Bikes show in Syracuse in 1987. While waiting for the show to begin, Mirra was riding flatland in the store's parking lot. Fred Blood, one of the company's pros, noticed Mirra, who was performing a difficult trick, called double decade, with the greatest of ease. The trick involved making two complete turns in midair while holding on to the handlebars. Mirra described the situation on *23mag.com*: "Not too many riders in the country were pulling that trick off at the time, so Fred was pretty surprised to see me, a five-foot-tall kid from Chittenango, pull one." The chance meeting brought Mirra his first sponsorship, which included a discount on a General bike and discounts on parts in exchange for riding in shows. It was a dream deal for any beginning BMXer.

Later that same year, Mirra accepted a better sponsorship by Haro. He got a couple bikes, some parts, and paid food and lodging at contests. Not a bad deal for a thirteen-year-old, small-town kid. Mirra's first competition, the AFA Masters, took place in October 1987. His nerves took over, and he finished in eleventh place, next to last. Mirra was dropped by Haro in 1988 due to financial cutbacks in the freestyle industry as a whole. Bike sales were down, and riders were being cut from nearly every team. Though disappointed, Mirra wasn't worried. His interests were changing, and his "career" soon took a new direction.

He explained to Scott Willoughby of the *Denver Post,* "I moved into ramp riding in the late '80s because I've always been more into jumping and taking risks. I think it was just something different than what everybody else was doing at my age. But I never really thought about it. That's just what I did." This is also around the time he met fellow BMXer Kevin Jones (1967–). Jones was part of a group called the Plywood Hoods. Mark Eaton (1969–) was another member of the Hoods. Mirra met Eaton at a contest in Pennsylvania when he was fourteen. Eaton invited Mirra to ride with the Hoods, a true honor for a kid who wanted nothing more than to ride BMX. The Plywood Hoods produced the first underground BMX video, *Dorkin' in York*. Mirra's friendship with Jones and Eaton landed him a spot

Plywood Hoods

First came the Cardboard Lords, a group of friends who rode BMX in the early 1980s, before freestyle became popular. The Cardboard Lords discovered breakdancing and spent the next year and a half perfecting their style. Kevin Jones was the leader of the pack; there were six other members.

By 1985, the Cardboard Lords had won all the local competitions, but breakdancing's popularity was dying out. Jones and another member, Mark Eaton, ran into an old friend one night. Mike Daily had a BMX freestyle team called the Plywood Hoods. The two Cardboard Lords were intrigued by what their friend was telling them about the Hoods, and two months later the Cardboard Lords disbanded. Jones, Eaton, and another member, Mark Dale, renewed their interest in BMX and began freestyling. They joined the Plywood Hoods.

Though the group specialized in flatland, the Hoods also continued to enjoy freestyle. Soon they were featured in a magazine article that publicized their attitude: We do what we want and don't care who or what might get in our way. The Hoods became instant heroes of the underground freestyle scene. Here was a group of average kids, with bikes that had been put together with spare parts. They were much more accessible to the underground scene than were the BMX "stars" of the day.

Dissatisfied with the instructional videos available on the market, the Plywood Hoods decided to make a video for freestylers. The Hoods took their own cameras around their hometown of York, Pennsylvania, and shot the movie themselves. Ever the humble teens, they called their film *Dorkin' in York*. The flick contained interviews with a number of riders with various styles. Music was incorporated, and before they knew it, the Plywood Hoods found themselves with a million-dollar-a-year industry. In 1990, the Hoods held the first York Jam, a noncompetitive riding session.

Throughout the 1990s riders from across the globe would move to York just to be part of the riding scene. All in all, there is a total of ten *Dorkin' in York* videos. They are available as a box set.

in *Dorkin' in York 2*. That invitation marked his debut into videos. It was merely a sign of things to come.

By 1989, Mirra was getting a reputation as a kid who had a serious future in BMX. He entered a Pennsylvania competition that summer, one in which there were no age divisions for amateurs in King of Vert(ical) events. So Mirra found himself competing against bikers in their twenties. He was just fifteen when he placed an impressive eighth out of twenty-five competitors. September found him in yet another King of Vert contest, this time in New York. He not only performed well, but landed a spot on the Dyno team when pro Dino DeLuca told his manager to sign Mirra. The deal meant more free bikes and all-expenses-paid travel.

Turns pro

The Dyno move proved to be a good one. Mirra finished seventh in the Expert class of the 1989 King of Vert finals. Soon he was touring the United States. In 1992, at the age of seventeen, Mirra turned pro. That summer he was featured on the June cover of *Invert* magazine and interviewed in the July *BMX Plus!* His sponsors included Hoffman Bikes, Airwalk, Homeless, and Standard Bikes. That was also the year Mirra invented some of his more famous tricks, including the backside weasel and frame-stand peg-pick.

One of Mirra's greatest moments came a year later when he beat freestyle champion Mat Hoffman in a half-pipe contest. It was Hoffman's first loss in three years. The freestyle industry hit a dry spell right after that feat. Supporters were pulling out and riders were on their own. Though the future looked bleak, Mirra continued to ride hard and dedicate his heart to the sport.

Life changed drastically in December 1993, when Mirra was hit by a drunk driver while crossing the street. The accident left the athlete with a fractured skull and torn shoulder. A blod clot formed in his brain, and no one was sure if Mirra would live. Recovery was maddeningly slow; it took six months of medication and time off from riding for Mirra to even begin to get his groove back. He told Willoughby, "It was a setback, but something I overcame. It doesn't even mess with me at all. In life there are obstacles you have to go through. Whatever it is, you overcome it eventually." But even then, there was so little happening in BMX around the country that he found it difficult to get motivated. Mirra moved to California in hopes of a new scene but moved back to New York within two weeks. But being home didn't feel right either. Looking back, Mirra considers 1994 a year of professional crisis. "It took me that long to figure out not to give up," he wrote on *23mag.com*.

The one highlight of Mirra's career at that time was doing well at the Chicago Bicycle Stunt Series competition in 1994. He placed first in street and third in vert, worthwhile performances especially in light of the accident.

Moves to North Carolina

In the meantime, Mirra's big brother, Tim, had moved to Greenville, North Carolina, to attend college—and he lived right across the street from a BMX park. Mirra visited his brother a few times before deciding to join him. Tim's support and encouragement helped Mirra get back to the determined mindset that put him at the top of his game before the accident. And it was the first time he'd ridden seriously in fifteen months.

Mirra signed with Haro again in 1994. This time, he was paid $30,000 a year to ride in competitions, a definite step up from a free bike and travel expenses. Haro also helped Mirra build a vert ramp to practice on and get him back to competing form. Mirra eventually built a 15,000-square-foot training complex in an industrial park just outside Greenville. The "warehouse" is considered to be one of the best facilities of its kind.

Dominates the X Games

In late 1994, ESPN announced it would host the first-ever X Games the following year. Athletes would compete in twenty-seven events in nine categories, including biking. Mirra competed and took home the silver medal. The X Games helped bring the world of BMX to a much larger audience, and soon the bike world couldn't get enough of Mirra. He was featured on numerous magazine covers and in interviews, all the while continuing to compete and dominate. In 1996, Mirra earned the title of World Champion of the pro vert. He was the X Games street champion that year as well and placed second in the pro vert. Mirra signed with Reebok that year, a move that increased his visibility and popularity.

The rider continued to squash the competition in the X Games throughout the rest of the 1990s. Between 1997 and 2000, Mirra won eight gold medals at the X Games, setting a record that remains untouched. In 1999 Mirra appeared on *The Late Show with David Letterman.* "Being on Letterman was just a whole other level. It was crazy, it felt as good as winning the

Dave Mirra flies high during a demonstra-
tion event in the half-pipe at the 2005 UCI
BMX Supercross World Championships.
AP/Wide World Photos.

X Games!" he told *23mag.com*. But as good as 1999 was, it was just a foreshadowing of what 2000 would bring.

The year 2000 was a phenomenal year for the twenty-six-year-old athlete. Aside from the fact that he had his own line of bubble gum and cereal, Mirra enjoyed the success of his Dave Mirra Freestyle BMX video game. Released in September, the PlayStation® game sold more than 1.2 million units by April 2001. Mirra developed a strong identity with consumers, so much so that Dave Mirra Freestyle BMX 2 for the PlayStation 2® was released later that year. The games have also been released for GameBoy, X Box, and Sega Dreamcast systems.

As if that weren't enough, Mirra was one of two alternative sports athletes to be recognized as a notable sports icon in mainstream media. His media exposure alone reached $2.5 million.

Twenty-first century rider

The awards kept coming for Mirra throughout the early twenty-first century. He won the NORA Cup Ramp Rider of the Year award in 2001, 2002, and 2003. The award is voted on by fans of the sport, so to win the cup three years in a row was a huge honor for Mirra. "Awards like this let me know my riding gets appreciated by a lot of people and that makes me feel really good," he's quoted as saying on *23mag.com*.

By 2005, Mirra had won a total of eighteen medals in the X Games; thirteen of them are gold. He took home the gold in four BMX vert and park competitions as well, and became one of the most-recognized BMX faces in the media. Mirra has been the World Champion ten times over and has won virtually every other title known to the BMX world. His name commands the respect of his colleagues and the worship of Mirra-wanna-bes. In 2004 he was chosen by MTV to host the series *Real World/Road Rules: The Inferno*. With two seasons under his belt, he's proven to be a hit with the viewing audience.

Mirra won the ESPY Award for Best Male Action Sports Athlete in 2005. The star athlete was quoted in a press release as saying, "Of all the awards that I've won, this is the ultimate compliment because this came from the fans." In July 2005, Mirra had returned home from a nine-day road trip from Reno to Vancouver. He made the trip with a handful of friends who were working with him to film his first movie, *Sentenced to Life*. The purpose of the road trip was to stop at every skate park along the journey and film Mirra performing stunts and meeting local riders. Although as of 2005 there was no release date yet for the film, no one doubted that Mirra would publish it. He's done everything he's set his mind to. He explained the Mirra philosophy to Willoughby: "Anything you want to get better at is a commitment. Without commitment, there would be no success."

Mirra planned to marry his longtime girlfriend in November 2005. When he's not biking, he gets involved with several charities, including the Dream Factory, a foundation that grants wishes to critically ill children.

For More Information

Books

Mahaney, Ian. *Dave Mirra: Bicycle Stunt Riding Champion.* New York, NY: PowerKids Press, 2005.

Mirra, Dave. *Mirra Images.* New York, NY: Regan Books, 2003.

Rosenberg, Aaron. *Dave Mirra: BMX Superstar.* New York, NY: Rosen Publishing Group, 2004.

Periodicals

Willoughby, Scott. "Freestyle Rider Mirra Continuing to Push Limits." *Denver Post.* Reprinted online at *Jackson Hole Star Tribune.* http://www.jacksonholestartrib.com/articles/2005/07/08/sports/9d5e0163929cf74d87257038005966da.txt (accessed on August 8, 2005).

Web Sites

"Biker Dave Mirra Enjoying Life in Fast Lane." *MSNBC.com* (July 9, 2005). http://msnbc.msn.com/id/8488768/ (accessed on August 8, 2005).

"Dave Mirra." *Maxxis.com.* http://www.maxxis.com/products/bicycle/riders_profile_details.asp?id = 140 (accessed on August 8, 2005).

"Dave Mirra Biography." *Kidzworld.com.* http://www.kidzworld.com/site/p4868.htm (accessed on August 8, 2005).

Dave Mirra Official Web Site. http://www.davemirra.com (accessed on August 8, 2005).

"Dave Mirra Receives Honor." *Reflector.com* (July 17, 2005). http://www.reflector.com/sports/content/sports/stories/2005/07/17/20050717GDRdave_mirra.html (accessed on August 8, 2005).

"Plywood Hoods History." *Plywoodhoods.com.* http://plywoodhoods.com/main.html?history.html (accessed August 8, 2005).

Chad Michael Murray

August 24, 1981 • ***Buffalo, New York***

Actor

Chad Michael Murray moved easily from television into feature films thanks to his roles in highly rated teen dramas on the WB network such as *Dawson's Creek* and *One Tree Hill.* By the time he began appearing in box office successes opposite Lindsay Lohan (1986–) and Hilary Duff (1987–), Murray had emerged as the new teen heartthrob for his boyish good looks and appealing screen portrayals of the sensitive loner-type.

Suffers teasing for his clothes

On *One Tree Hill,* Murray had been cast as a teen from a struggling single-parent household, a situation that was not unlike the actor's own upbringing. Born in Buffalo, New York, in August 1981, he was the second of five children. His mother left the family when he was ten years old. Their father, Rex, an air traffic controller, raised them as a solo parent, and money was tight; Murray has said that he was a target for bullies because of the clothes he wore. By the time he was thirteen, he was working as a janitor in a doughnut shop to earn his own spending money.

At Clarence High School, outside of Buffalo, Murray played football, and one day on the field he suffered a bad hit to the stomach that put him in the hospital. A nurse suggested that he should model, and so Murray signed with a local agency, which eventually sent him to an industry event

> **"I've made decisions for me that some people may not see as proper decisions, but it works for me."**

in Orlando, Florida. There, a Hollywood talent scout told the seventeen-year-old Murray that he should move to California and try his luck in the entertainment business. Murray was already a film enthusiast and had a job at a local movie theater, where he was able to see small, well-crafted independent films. "That's when I really fell in love with great acting," Murray recalled about the high-school job in an interview with *Buffalo News* writer, Toni Ruberto. "I just wanted to do it and give it a shot."

Murray also may have been eager to leave certain things behind. When he was eighteen, his mother appeared at the Murray family doorstep after an absence of several years. "I answered the door, it was really uncomfortable," he told Alan Pergament in the *Buffalo News*. "I don't really have a relationship with her." That same year, in 1999, Murray graduated from Clarence High and used the money he had received as a graduation gift to fund his cross-country move. "I told myself that if nothing happened in a year, I'd go to college and play football," he said to *American Fitness* writer Bonnie Siegler.

Lives on cereal and fast food

Murray and his father made the cross-country road trip together, and then his father flew back home. Some of Murray's first solo weeks were spent at a Red Roof Inn, and he was determined to make his savings stretch as long as possible. "I had a dollar a day to buy a chicken sandwich or a salad from Jack in the Box [a fast food chain]," he told *Teen People*. "At the beginning of every week, I would buy milk and a box of cereal. Every morning and night I ate cereal, and during the day I would have a chicken sandwich. That was pretty much all I had. I bought a 19-inch TV that had, like, four channels, and one was the WB."

In the meantime, the talent scout Murray had met in Orlando helped him find an agent, who in turn helped him find a manager and an acting coach. Murray began to get some modeling work, appearing in ads for Tommy Hilfiger, Sketchers, and Gucci. But it was a visit to a fast-food restaurant that accidentally gave him his shot at stardom. At a Burger King, he was jumped by three guys, and his nose was broken. It was reset in the emergency room, and "a week later, I finally started getting work," he told Lauren Brown in a *CosmoGIRL!* interview. "Why? Because before that, I kept getting comments that my nose made me too 'pretty.'"

Murray made his television debut as Chad Murray in an episode of *Chicken Soup for the Soul*, the feel-good PAX TV drama. In the show, he played a rich teenager who doesn't like his own family. In 2000, he went on an audition for a WB pilot, *Day One*, and though the show never went into production, WB executives thought Murray had potential and signed him to a development deal. He was cast as another rich kid, Tristan DuGrey, in the first season of *Gilmore Girls*, a new sitcom. The show centered on the mother-daughter relationship between teenage Rory, played by Alexis Bledel (1981–), and her single mom, played by Lauren Graham (1967–). Murray was cast as

Rory's arrogant classmate and romantic interest when she starts a new school year at an elite private academy.

Turns down *O.C.* part

In the 2001–02 television season, Murray appeared in several episodes of *Dawson's Creek,* a hit teen drama. He played college student and budding rock star Charlie Todd, who becomes romantically involved with both Joey Potter, played by Katie Holmes (1978–), as well as her friend, Jen, played by Michelle Williams (1980–), when both teenagers begin college in Boston. Murray was also cast in the title role in a WB television movie, *The Lone Ranger,* as well as starring in the television series *One Tree Hill.*

Murray was actually up for two parts at the time and had to choose between the WB show and a new one on Fox in which he was also offered a lead. The part he turned down was that of *The O.C.*'s Ryan Atwood, a troubled teen who is rescued by a kind lawyer and finds himself unexpectedly living in a posh community in Orange County, California. The show was a tremendous hit immediately upon its Fox debut in August 2003, winning both a devoted teen audience as well as older viewers thanks to its melodramatic storylines and alternative-music soundtrack. "Don't want to go into that," he said when asked about the decision by *New York Times* writer Kate Aurthur on the set of *One Tree Hill.* "This one felt like home to me."

One Tree Hill also debuted in the fall new-series line-up of 2003, but unlike its Fox counterpart, pulled in terrible ratings in its early weeks. Murray played Lucas "Luke" Scott, a teen from a single-parent household in a small North Carolina town called Tree Hill. Luke is a talented basketball player who finds himself competing with a new star on his high school team, an arrogant rich kid named Nathan who also turns out to be his half-brother. Luke's father, who he never knew, left his mother when their high school romance produced an unplanned pregnancy. His dad went to college on a basketball scholarship, got married, and had another child soon after leaving Tree Hill. He returns to

Chad Michael Murray, Elisha Cuthbert, and Paris Hilton (right) pose with director Jaume Collet-Serra (far left) at the premiere of their 2005 film House of Wax. © Fred Prouser/Reuters/Corbis.

become a successful business leader and puts his thwarted basketball ambitions on his second son, Nathan—Luke's new teammate. The two sons—one coddled, the other shunned—find themselves competing on the basketball court. A romantic rivalry grows when Luke hits it off with Nathan's moody, punk-rock girlfriend, Peyton (Hilarie Burton). "I liked how introverted the character was," Murray said of the role of Luke in an interview with the *Buffalo News*. "He's very torn between his father, his mother and his brother. And I liked the family dynamic. It's a very interesting one. I've lived a little of that, so I felt like I had the opportunity to explore that even further and explain to a young audience."

Teens tuned in

One Tree Hill had a much better second season, scoring a number one spot in prime-time ratings among teenage girls on Tuesday nights. Some of the new interest came from Murray's heartthrob status, and also because the show's writers and producers began to play up the romantic competition between the two half-brothers.

In 2003, Murray also appeared in a highly anticipated feature film, *Freaky Friday*. He played Jake, the romantic interest somewhat confused by the switched-identity premise that fuels the plot of this teen comedy. *Freaky Friday* did well at the box office in the summer of 2003, and Murray's performance earned a good mention in *Variety*. "As Jake finds himself, much to his perplexity, equally attracted to Anna's 'mother,' Murray offers a textbook example of how to grab attention while engagingly underplaying," wrote critic Joe Leydon.

Murray appeared opposite another teen-screen queen in *A Cinderella Story*, which was released in 2004. This time, he played the "prince" who falls in love with Hilary Duff's character. Several months later, in the spring of 2005, he played the on-screen twin brother of Elisha Cuthbert (1982–) in his first horror flick, *House of Wax*. The movie was a remake of a classic horror film from 1953 that starred Vincent Price, which itself was the second filmed version of the 1933 original, *Mystery of the Wax Museum*. The characters played by Murray and Cuthbert were part of a group of teens who come across a creepy, deserted town in which they find dead bodies covered in wax. Other castmates included Murray's friend and former *Gilmore Girls* actor, Jared Padalecki (1982–), and hotel-chain heiress Paris Hilton (1981–).

Marries costar

Murray became a teen heartthrob thanks to the success of *One Tree Hill* and the well-publicized films with Lohan and Duff. But the hit WB series, which began its third season in 2005, also served to remove him from the Hollywood celebrity-dating pool. He became involved with his *One Tree Hill* costar Sophia Bush, and

A Hollywood Ending

When Sophia Bush met her future husband on the set of the WB teen drama *One Tree Hill,* in which she had just been cast, she was a relative newcomer to the entertainment industry. She had spent the prior three years involved in her studies at the University of South California (USC) where she majored in journalism with a minor in theater. She had also worked for a student news service, been active in the USC chapter of the Kappa Kappa Gamma sorority, and was chosen as the Tournament of Roses Parade Queen in 2000, the annual New Year's Day parade before the college football Rose Bowl game. "My life was crazy," she recalled in an interview with *In Style* writer Rory Evans, "and I had never seen Chad on *Dawson's Creek* or *Gilmore Girls.* I had no idea whatsoever about the scope of his teen-idol status."

Born on July 8, 1982, Bush grew up in Pasadena, California, the home of the Rose Bowl since 1890. She attended a private school for girls in Pasadena, and while still at USC had won a small role in the 2002 feature film *Van Wilder.* After reporting to the set for a role in *Terminator 3* she was recast because the director decided she looked too young for the part.

Bush and Murray began dating almost immediately after they met in 2003. The following spring, she traveled to visit him on the set of *House of Wax*, being shot in Australia. He proposed to her the day she arrived. They were wed in Santa Monica, California, the following April, and both went back to work almost immediately. In 2005 Bush was filming a 2006 thriller titled *Stay Alive.* The newlyweds were still castmates on *One Tree Hill* and shared a

Sophia Bush. © Vaughn Youtz / Zuma / Corbis.

house in Wilmington, North Carolina, where the series was filmed. As she recalled in the *In Style* interview, Bush knew when they met that it was a good casting call. "It was like I knew exactly who I was staring at," she told Evans, "and I saw him get this weird look too. We were on the same page."

the pair wed in April 2005 at the Hotel Casa Del Mar in Santa Monica, California, with the Pacific Ocean as the scenic backdrop for the ceremony. The *House of Wax* premiere and required round of publicity appearances and magazine interviews for Murray meant they had to postpone their honeymoon until later that year. He admitted in some articles that it had not been easy to date a co-worker at first. They tried to keep it secret on the WB set, he said, "for about a month because we didn't know exactly how everyone was going to react," he confessed to Brown. "And we wanted to be sure that we were going to be serious as a couple. But when we knew this was real, we got sick of keeping it from everyone."

Murray was cast in his first motion picture lead role for a 2006 movie, *Stealing Cars*. The story centers around a troubled teen who lands in a brutal juvenile-detention facility. "It's a great story," he told Toni Ruberto in a *Buffalo News* interview. "It's very emotional and physical."

With a long career ahead of him—perhaps even one in which he moves from teen celebrity-hunk into serious drama, Murray is humble about his ambitions. For his future, he told Siegler in *American Fitness,* he hopes for "health, happiness, a family, a nice house, a dog and a few restaurants—basically slowing everything down and taking stress out of life. I already have ideas for three restaurants," he said, with one of them being a deli that would sell "my signature meal—a pepperoni and bacon sandwich." His father is the person he admires most, he told *Teen People*. "The fact that he worked full-time and got dinner on the table every night is an amazing thing," he asserted. "Having him as a role model makes you realize you've got to work for what you want."

For More Information

Periodicals

Armstrong, Jennifer, Rebecca Ascher-Walsh, and Kristen Baldwin. "19 Chad Michael Murray: Television." *Entertainment Weekly* (June 25, 2004): p. 71.

Aurthur, Kate. "Teenage Girls Lift Soapy Drama from Slump." *New York Times* (January 25, 2005): p. E1.

Brown, Lauren. "Chad Michael Murray." *CosmoGIRL!* (May 2004): p. 158.

"Chad Michael Murray (Star/Flashback)." *Teen People* (April 1, 2005): p. 146.

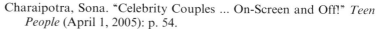

Charaipotra, Sona. "Celebrity Couples ... On-Screen and Off!" *Teen People* (April 1, 2005): p. 54.

Evans, Rory. "One Sweet Thrill." *In Style* (April 4, 2005): p. 148.

Goober, Lesley. "Chad Michael Murray (Hunk of the Month)." *Cosmopolitan* (June 2004): p. 80.

Heffernan, Virginia. "Mismatched Lovers and Contrasting Brothers." *New York Times* (September 23, 2003): p. E8.

Leydon, Joe. "Surprising Fun in Cheeky 'Freaky.'" *Variety* (July 28, 2003): p. 27.

Pergament, Alan. "Clarence Actor Sports Experience in Series Role." *Buffalo News* (July 17, 2003): p. B5.

"The Real Thing." *People* (May 2, 2005): p. 75.

Ruberto, Toni. "Making the Climb." *Buffalo News* (May 1, 2005): p. G1.

Schaefer, Stephen. "Chad Michael Murray Looks for a Career Boost from 'House of Wax.'" *Boston Herald* (May 1, 2005): p. 31.

Siegler, Bonnie. "Hollywood Bound." *American Fitness* (March–April 2002): p. 16.

Smith, Jennifer L. "We Love Chad." *Teen People* (September 1, 2004): p. 138.

Wheat, Alynda. "Teenage Wasteland." *Entertainment Weekly* (February 20, 2004): p. 54.

Web Sites

One Tree Hill. http://www.thewb.com/Shows/Show/0,7353,||1490,00.html (accessed on August 23, 2005).

Elon Musk

1971 • South Africa

Entrepreneur, philanthropist

Elon Musk was a multi-millionaire by the time he reached the age of thirty-one thanks to his creation of the company that became PayPal, the popular money-transfer service for Web consumers. Musk has become one of a new breed of what the *New York Times* called "thrillionaires," or a class of former high-tech entrepreneurs who are using their newfound wealth to help turn science-fiction dreams into reality. Musk is the founder of Space Exploration Technologies, or SpaceX, a company based in El Segundo, California. In 2005 SpaceX was busy building the Falcon rocket, which he hoped could some day make both space tourism and a colony on the planet Mars realistic goals for humankind.

Sells homemade video game

Musk is a native of South Africa, born in 1971 to parents who later divorced. His father was an engineer and his mother—originally from Canada—was a nutritionist. Musk was fascinated by science fiction and computers in his adolescent years. When he was twelve, he wrote the code for his own video game and actually sold it to a company. In his late teens, he immigrated to Canada in order to avoid the required military service for white males in South Africa. It was still the era of apartheid, the South African legal system that denied political and economic rights to the country's majority-black native population. Musk was uninterested in serving in the army, which was engaged at the time in a battle to stamp out a black nationalist movement. Thanks to his mother's Canadian ties, he was able to

> "Failure is an option here. If things are not failing, you are not innovating enough."

enroll at Queen's University in Kingston, one of Ontario's top schools.

Musk had planned on a career in business, and he worked at a Canadian bank one summer as a college intern. This was his only real job before he became an Internet entrepreneur. Midway through his undergraduate education, he transferred to the University of Pennsylvania, where he earned a bachelor's degree in economics and a second bachelor's in physics a year later. From there, he won admission to the prestigious doctoral program at Stanford University in California, where he planned to concentrate on a Ph.D. in energy physics. He moved to California just as the Internet boom was starting in 1995, and he decided he wanted to be in on it, too. He dropped out of Stanford after just two days in order to start his first company, Zip2 Corporation. This was an online city guide aimed at the newspaper publishing business, and Musk was able to land contracts with both the *New York Times* and the *Chicago Tribune* to provide content for their new online sites.

Musk was just twenty-four when he started the company, and he devoted all of his energies to see it succeed. At one point, he lived in the same rented office that served as his company's headquarters, sleeping on a futon couch and showering at the local YMCA, which "was cheaper than renting an apartment," he explained in an interview with Roger Eglin of the *Sunday Times* of London. Still, the company struggled to fulfill its contracts and meet the payroll and other costs, and he looked for outside financing. Eventually a group of venture capitalists, investors who provide start-up money to new businesses, financed Zip2 with $3.6 million, but he gave up majority control of the company in exchange.

Starts online bank

In the end, Musk's decision was a smart one. In February 1999 Compaq Computer Corporation bought Zip2 for $307 million in cash, which was one of the largest cash deals in the Internet business sector at the time. Out of that amount, Musk was paid $22 million for his 7 percent share, which made him a millionaire at twenty-eight. In 1999, he used $10 million of it to start another company, which he called X.com. This was an online bank with grand plans to become a full-range provider of financial services to consumers. The company's one major innovation was figuring out how to securely transfer money using a recipient's e-mail address.

Musk's proven track record from Zip2 helped it gain serious attention and generous investors right away. Two important executives signed on with him: investment banker John Story and Bill Harris, the former chief executive officer of Intuit Corporation, the maker of the best-selling Quicken accounting software as well as TurboTax, a tax-preparation program. Harris was appointed president and chief executive officer of X.com, with Musk serving as company chair. The company received a generous infusion of $25 million in start-up capital from Sequoia Capital, a leading venture-capital firm in California.

X.com went online in December 1999 with a bold offer for new customers: those who opened an online checking account with X.com received a $20 cash card that they could use at an automatic-teller machine (ATM). If they referred a friend, they received a $10 card for each new member who signed up. Within two months, X.com had one hundred thousand customers, which was close to the number reached by its major competitor, Etrade Telebank. But consumer skepticism about the security of online banking was X.com's biggest obstacle to success, and there was a setback when Musk and the other executives had to admit that computer hackers had been able to perform some illegal transfers from traditional bank accounts into X.com accounts. They immediately started a new policy that required customers to submit a canceled check in order to withdraw money, but there were tensions in the office about the future of the company.

Buys PayPal

In March 2000, X.com bought a company called Confinity, which had started an Internet money-transfer presence called PayPal. PayPal was originally set up to let users of handheld personal digital assistants, or PDAs, transfer money. It had only been in business a few months when X.com acquired it, and Musk believed that its online-transfer technology, which was known as "P2P" for "person-to-person," had a promising future. He and Harris did not agree, and Harris resigned from X.com in May 2000. Five months later, Musk announced that X.com would abandon its original online bank and instead concentrate on turning itself into the leading global payment transfer provider. The X.com name was dropped in favor of PayPal.

PayPal grew enormously through 2001, thanks in part to its presence on eBay, the online auction Web site where person-to-person sales were happening in the hundreds of thousands. When PayPal became a publicly traded company with an initial public offering (IPO) of stock in February 2002, it had an impressive debut on the first day of Wall Street trading. Later that year, eBay bought the company outright for $1.5 billion. At the time, Musk was PayPal's largest shareholder, holding an 11.5 percent stake, and he netted $165 million in valuable eBay stock from the deal.

By then Musk had already moved on to his next venture. In June 2002 he founded SpaceX, or Space Exploration Technologies. He had long been fascinated by the possibility of life on Mars and was a member of the Mars Society, a nonprofit organization that encourages the exploration of the red planet. Filmmaker James Cameron (1954–) is one of several notable Mars Society members. Musk wanted to create a "Mars Oasis," sending an experimental greenhouse to the planet, which in favorable alignment of the planets is about 35 million miles distant from Earth. His oasis would contain a nutrient gel from which specific Mars-environment-friendly plant life could grow. His plan had a cost of $20 million. But then he learned that to send something into space with the standard delivery method, a Delta rocket made by the Boeing Corporation, would add another $50 million to the cost. Musk even tried to buy a rocket from Russia, but realized that dealing with the somewhat suspect international traders who dealt in such underground, or illegal, items was just too risky.

Borrows *Star Wars* name

Musk thought that maybe he might be able to build his own rocket instead. He began contacting innovators and technicians in the American aerospace industry, and he managed to lure some experienced engineers and technical specialists away from companies like Boeing and TRW to come and work for him at SpaceX's headquarters in El Segundo, California. He had a much more difficult time attracting venture capital for this idea, however. "Space is pretty far out of the comfort zone of just about every VC on Earth," he admitted to Matt Marshall of the *San Jose Mercury News*. Instead, he was forced to put up his own money to build what would become the first reusable rocket in the private sector.

Musk and his new SpaceX team began to build two types of Falcon rockets. The name came from the "Millennium Falcon," the spacecraft in the *Star Wars* movies. The plan was to build a rocket by using existing technology and at the lowest possible cost. The Falcon I, for example, uses a pintle engine, which dates from the 1960s. It has one fuel injector, while standard rockets used by the U.S. National Aeronautics and Space Administration (NASA) generally use what is known as a "showerhead" design that features several fuel injectors. The company also needed a theodolite, which is used to align rockets, and instead of buying it new, they saved $25,000 by finding one on eBay.

The New "Thrillionaires"

Microsoft co-founder Paul Allen (1953–) is ranked the seventh richest person in the world. Allen has used his wealth to finance *SpaceShipOne*. This private manned spacecraft, built by aircraft design pioneer Burt Rutan (1943–), was the first of its kind to reach suborbital space twice, which it did in 2004. For this two-time achievement, *SpaceShipOne* met the conditions of the $10 million Ansari X prize, established by the X Prize Foundation to encourage private entrepreneurship in aerospace.

Doom video game co-creator **John Carmack** (1970–; see entry) founded a computer game development company called id Software in 1991. He is considered one of the most gifted programmers ever to work in the gaming industry. He was one of the creators of the successful *Doom* and *Quake* games, which sold millions in the 1990s and attracted legions of devoted fans. In 2000, Carmack funded a new venture, Armadillo Aerospace in Mesquite, Texas, with the goal of building a manned suborbital spacecraft. It lost its bid to win the Ansari X prize when its vehicles ran into technical problems and crashed in 2004 and 2005.

Paul Allen. Mike Blake/Reuters/Landov.

In 1995, Jeff Bezos (1964–) launched Amazon.com, an online bookseller that became one of the most impressive successes in American business history. With an estimated personal fortune of over $5 billion, Bezos began donating some of his wealth to various philanthropic causes, but he also established an aerospace company. His Blue Origin, like Allen and Carmack's ventures, is also committed to manned suborbital space flight. His project is to be propelled by a mixture of hydrogen peroxide and kerosene and is a vertical-takeoff and landing-vehicle.

There are other, equally expensive costs associated with rocketry. Since Musk's design would be reusable, the company needed to get back the rocket's first stage, which the rocket sheds as it leaves the Earth's atmosphere. The part usually falls into the ocean, according to safety plans, but retrieval at sea is expensive.

Companies that contract with NASA charge $250,000 to bring such parts back, but Musk found some ocean-salvage companies that knew how to handle sensitive material. He found one that agreed to do the job for just $60,000. The Falcon does not have a specialty computer on board, which can cost $1 million alone to install and maintain. Instead its computer is a basic one that uses the same technology as an automatic teller machine and costs just $5,000.

Envisions Hondas in space

By building a reliable rocket at an affordable cost, SpaceX hopes to be able to take small satellites into orbit for a fee of around $6 million. This is half the standard rate in the aerospace business to take something into space. The company already had two customers—the U.S. Department of Defense and the government of Malaysia. "Many times we've been asked, 'If you reduce the cost, don't you reduce reliability?' This is completely ridiculous," Musk explained to *Fast Company* writer Jennifer Reingold. "A Ferrari is a very expensive car. It is not reliable. But I would bet you 1,000-to-1 that if you bought a Honda Civic that that sucker will not break down in the first year of operation. You can have a cheap car that's reliable, and the same applies to rockets."

Musk serves as the chief technology officer of SpaceX. All employees are shareholders, and the company's casual but committed atmosphere is reinforced by the workday presence of Musk's four dogs. He no longer sleeps at the office, however, for he has a home, a wife there, and in the garage a McLaren F1, a $1.2 million car that is the fastest production, or non-customized race car, in the world. He has testified before members of the U.S. Congress on the possibility of commercial human space flight and has also established the Musk Foundation, which is committed to space exploration and the discovery of clean energy sources. The Foundation runs the Musk Mars Desert Observatory telescope in southern Utah, as well as a simulated Mars environment where visitors can experience what life on Mars might be like, including waste-burning toilets. "I think human exploration of space is very important," he told Reingold. "Certainly, from a survival standpoint, the probability of living longer is much greater if we're on more than one planet."

For More Information

Periodicals

Corcoran, Elizabeth. "Something Better than Free." *Forbes* (February 21, 2000): p. 62b.

Eglin, Roger. "Silicon Valley Shows How to Reach Stars." *Sunday Times* (London, England) (December 1, 2002): p. 7.

Lubove, Seth. "Way Out There." *Forbes* (May 12, 2003): p. 138.

Marshall, Matt. "Venture Capital Column." *San Jose Mercury News* (July 13, 2004).

Ptacek, Megan J. "X.com Scraps Bank Strategy to Focus on PayPal System." *American Banker* (October 11, 2000): p. 1.

Reingold, Jennifer. "Hondas in Space." *Fast Company* (February 2005): p. 74.

Schwartz, John. "Thrillionaires: The New Space Capitalists." *New York Times* (June 14, 2005): p. F1.

Wallace, Nora K. "Vandenberg Air Base, Calif., to Launch SpaceX Reusable Rocket in January." *Santa Barbara News-Press* (October 5, 2003).

Web Sites

The Mars Society. http://www.marssociety.org/ (accessed on August 23, 2005).

Space Exploration Technologies Corporation. http://www.spacex.com/ (accessed on August 23, 2005).

Barack Obama

August 4, 1961 • *Honolulu, Hawaii*

Politician

Illinois voters sent a Democratic newcomer, Barack Obama, to one of the state's two seats in the U.S. Senate in 2004. Obama's landslide victory in Illinois was significant on several fronts. Firstly, he became the Senate's only African American lawmaker when he was sworn into office in January 2005, and just the third black U.S. senator to serve there since the 1880s. Moreover, Obama's political supporters came from a diverse range of racial and economic backgrounds, which is still relatively rare in American electoral politics—traditionally, black candidates have not done very well in voting precincts where predominantly non-minority voters go to the polls. Even before his Election Day victory, Obama emerged as the new star of the Democratic Party after delivering the keynote address at the Democratic National Convention in Boston, Massachusetts that summer. His stirring speech, in which he urged a united, not a divided, American union, prompted political commentators to predict he might become the first African American elected to the White House.

Born in Hawaii

Obama is actually of mixed heritage. He was born in 1961 in Honolulu, Hawaii, where his parents had met at the University of Hawaii's Manoa campus. His father, Barack Sr., was from Kenya and entered the University of Hawaii as its first-ever student from an African country. He was a member of Kenya's Luo ethnic group, many of whom played a key role in that country's struggle for independence in the 1950s. Obama's mother, Ann Durham, was originally from Kansas, where some of her ancestors had been anti-slavery activists in the 1800s.

"In no other country on earth is my story even possible."

The marriage between Obama's parents was a short-lived one, however. In the early 1960s, interracial relationships were still quite rare in many parts of America, and even technically illegal in some states. The Durhams were accepting of Barack Sr., but his family in Kenya had a harder time with the idea of his marrying a white American woman. When Obama was two years old they divorced, and his father left Hawaii to enter Harvard University to earn a Ph.D. in economics. The two Baracks met again only once, when Obama was ten, though they did write occasionally. Barack Sr. eventually returned to Kenya and died in a car accident there in the early 1980s.

Obama's mother remarried a man from Indonesia who worked in the oil industry, and when Obama was six they moved there. The family lived near the capital of Jakarta, where his half-sister Maya was born. At the age of ten, Obama returned to Hawaii and lived with his maternal grandparents; later his mother and sister returned as well. Called "Barry" by his family and friends, he was sent to a prestigious private academy in Honolulu, the Punahou School, where he was one of just a handful of black students. Obama recalled feeling conflicted about his mixed heritage in his teen years. Outside the house, he was considered African American, but the only family he knew was his white one at home. For a time, he loafed and let his grades slip; instead of studying, he spent hours on the basketball court with his friends, and has admitted that there was a time when he experimented with drugs, namely marijuana and cocaine. "I was affected by the problems that I think a lot of young African American teens have," he reflected in an interview with Kenneth Meeks for *Black Enterprise*. "They feel that they need to rebel against society as a way of proving their blackness. And often, this results in self-destructive behavior."

Excels at Harvard Law School

Obama graduated from Punahou and went on to Occidental College in Los Angeles, where he decided to get serious about his studies. Midway through, he transferred to the prestigious Columbia University in New York City. He also began to explore his African roots and not long after his father's death traveled to meet his relatives in Kenya for the first time. After he earned his undergraduate degree in political science, he became a community organizer in Harlem—but quickly realized he could not afford to live in the city with a job that paid so little. Instead, he moved to Chicago to work for a church-based social-services organization there. The group was active on the city's South Side, one of America's most impoverished urban communities.

Feeling it was time to move on, Obama applied to and was accepted at Harvard Law School, one of the top three law schools in the United States. In 1990, he was elected president of the *Harvard Law Review* journal. He was the first African American to serve in the post, which virtually assured him of any career path he chose after graduation. But Obama declined the job offers from top Manhattan law firms, with their starting salaries that neared the $100,000-a-year range, in order to return to Chicago and work for a small firm that specialized in civil-rights law. This was an especially unglamorous and modest-paying field of law, for it involved defending the poor and the marginalized members of society in housing and employment discrimination cases.

Obama also had another reason for returning to Chicago: During his Harvard Law School years, he took a job as a summer associate at a Chicago firm, and the attorney assigned to mentor him was also a Harvard Law graduate, Michelle Robinson. The two began dating and were married in 1992. Robinson came from a working-class black family and grew up on the South Side; her brother had excelled at basketball and went to Princeton University, and she followed him there for her undergraduate degree. Obama also considered Chicago a place from which he could launch a political career, and he became active in a number of projects in addition to his legal cases at work and another job he held teaching classes at the University of Chicago Law School. He worked on a local voter-registration drive, for example, that registered thousands of black voters in Chicago; the effort was said to have helped Bill Clinton (1946–) win the state in his successful bid for the White House in 1992.

Writes autobiography

Obama's time at the Law Review had netted him an offer to write a book. The result was *Dreams from My Father: A Story of Race and Inheritance,* published by Times Books in 1995. The work merited some brief but mostly complimentary reviews in the press. Obama, however, was not hoping for a career as an author: he decided to run for a seat in the Illinois state senate. He ran from his home district of Hyde Park, the neighborhood surrounding the elite University of Chicago on the South Side. Though Hyde Park is similar to many American college towns, with well-kept homes and upscale businesses, the surrounding neighborhood is a more traditionally urban one, with higher levels of both crime and unemployment.

Obama won that 1996 election and went on to an impressive career in the Senate chambers in Springfield, the state capital. He championed a bill that gave tax breaks to low-income families, worked to expand a state health-insurance program for uninsured children, and wrote a bill that required law enforcement officials in every community to begin keeping track of their traffic stops and noting the race of the driver. This controversial bill, which passed thanks to Obama's determined effort to find support from

Black Senators in U.S. History

Barack Obama became the fifth African American senator in U.S. history in 2005. He was only the third elected since the end of the Reconstruction, the period immediately following the end of the American Civil War (1861–65; a war between the Union [the North], who were opposed to slavery, and the Confederacy [the South], who were in favor of slavery). During the Reconstruction Era, federal troops occupied the defeated Southern states and, along with transplanted government officials, one of their duties was to make sure that newly freed slaves were allowed to vote fairly and freely in elections.

Before 1913 and the passage of the Seventeenth Amendment to the U.S. Constitution, members of the U.S. Senate were not directly elected by voters in most states, however. Instead they were elected by legislators in the state assemblies, or appointed by the governor. Still, because of the Reconstruction Era reforms, many blacks were elected to the state legislatures that sent senators to Washington. In 1870, the Mississippi state legislature made Hiram Rhoades Revels (1827–1901) the state's newest senator and the first black ever to serve in the U.S. Senate. Revels was a free-born black from North

Carolina and a distinguished minister in the African Methodist Episcopal Church who had raised two black regiments that fought on the Union side during the Civil War. He served in the Senate for one year.

In 1875, Mississippi lawmakers sent Blanche K. Bruce (1841–1898) to the U.S. Senate. A former slave from Virginia, Bruce was a teacher and founder of the first school for blacks in the state of Missouri. After the end of the Civil War, he headed south to take part in the Reconstruction Era. He won election to local office as a Republican, and in 1875 lawmakers sent him to the U.S. Senate. He served the full six-year term. In 1881, he was appointed a U.S. Treasury official, and his signature was the first from an African American to appear on U.S. currency.

Nearly a hundred years passed before another African American was elected to the Senate, and this came by statewide vote. Edward William Brooke III (1919–), a Republican from Massachusetts, was elected to the U.S. Senate in 1966 and served two terms. In 1992 another Illinois Democrat, Carol Moseley Braun (1947–), became the first African American woman to serve in the U.S. Senate.

both political parties in the state Senate, was aimed at reducing incidents of alleged racial profiling, or undue suspicion turned upon certain minority or ethnic groups by police officers on patrol. He also won passage of another important piece of legislation that required police to videotape homicide confessions.

Obama made his first bid for U.S. Congress in 2000, when he challenged a well-known black politician and former Chicago City Council member, Bobby Rush (1946–), for his seat in the U.S. House of Representatives. Rush was a former

Barack Obama won his bid for the Senate by a large margin, taking 70 percent of the Illinois vote, thus becoming one of the youngest members of the U.S. Senate when he was sworn into office in January 2005. © Brooks Kraft/Corbis.

1960s radical who had founded the Illinois chapter of the Black Panther Party, a revolutionary black nationalist party of the era. Rush's campaign stressed his experience and questioned Obama's support base among wealthier white voters in the city, and Obama was solidly defeated in the primary, winning just 30 percent of the vote.

Enters Senate race

A few years later, Obama decided to run for a seat in the U.S. Senate when Illinois Republican Peter G. Fitzgerald (1960–) announced he would retire. Some of Obama's supporters thought he was aiming too high, but this time he beat out six other Democratic challengers in the primary with 53 percent of the vote. Suddenly, state and even national Democratic Party leaders began taking him and his Senate campaign seriously.

In the primary, he had managed to do what few African American politicians had ever done: record an impressive number of votes from precincts that had a predominantly white population.

In his 2004 Senate race, Obama faced a tough Republican challenger, however: a former investment banker turned parochial-school (school supported by a church parish) teacher named Jack Ryan (1960–). Ryan was blessed with television-actor good looks and had even once been married to *Boston Public* star Jeri Ryan (1968–). But Jack Ryan was, like one of Obama's earlier primary opponents, derailed by allegations about his personal life. Chicago news outlets publicized Ryan's divorce documents from 1999, which revealed one or two incidents that seemed distinctly at odds with a Republican "family values" platform. Ryan dropped out of the race, but the Republican National Party quickly brought in talk-show host Alan Keyes (1950–), who changed his home address from Maryland to Illinois to run against Obama. Keyes was a conservative black Republican who twice had made a bid for the White House, but he worried some voters with his strong statements against homosexuality.

Obama, by contrast, was winning public-opinion polls among every demographic group that pollsters asked. He was even greeted with rock-star type cheers in rural Illinois farm towns. Many of these small-town voters recognized that the manufacturing operations of many U.S. industries were rapidly being moved overseas thanks to free-trade agreements that eliminated tariffs (taxes) and trade barriers between the United States and Mexico; another free-trade agreement was in the works for Central America. The result was a dramatic decline in U.S. manufacturing jobs. Obama's campaign pledged to stop the outsourcing of such jobs to overseas facilities. But Obama suddenly found himself in the national spotlight, when John Kerry (1943–), expected to win the Democratic Party's nomination for president at the Democratic National Convention in July 2004, asked Obama to deliver the convention's keynote address. The keynote speech is expected to set the tone of the political campaign, and those chosen to give face tremendous expectations.

"That makes my life poorer"

Obama did not disappoint that evening. His speech, which he wrote himself and titled "The Audacity of Hope," was stirring and eloquent, and quickly dubbed by political analysts to be one of the best convention keynote addresses of the modern era. He earned several standing ovations during it, and Obama's confident, assured tone was broadcast to the rest of the nation. Cameras occasionally scanned the crowd to show tears on the faces of delegates. Obama praised Kerry's values and experience, and he reminded delegates and the national television audience that the country's strength came from unity, not division—that Americans had created a thriving nation out of many diverse ethnic groups and ideologies in its 228-year history. Economic policies aimed at providing a better life for everyone, not just a privileged few, was the American way, he said. "If there's a senior citizen somewhere who can't pay for her prescription and has to choose between medicine and the rent, that makes my life poorer, even if it's not my grandmother," he told the crowd. "If there's an Arab American family being rounded up without benefit of an attorney or due process, that threatens my civil liberties. It's that fundamental belief—I am my brother's keeper, I am my sister's keeper—that makes this country work."

Obama's speech, analysts said almost immediately, struck a hopeful, healing tone for a drastically divided nation and what had become a bitter, insult-heavy presidential contest. Obama, asserted *Time*'s Amanda Ripley, "described a country that America wants very badly to be: a country not pockmarked by racism and fear or led by politicians born into privilege and coached into automatons [robotic behavior]." Others called it one of the best political speeches of the century. Some newspaper and magazine editorial writers predicted that the rising star from Illinois would emerge a strong leader in the Democratic Party over the next few years, and could even run for president in 2012 or 2016.

Obama won his bid for the Senate a few months later by a large margin, taking 70 percent of the Illinois vote against just 27 percent for Keyes. At just forty-three years old, he became one of the youngest members of the U.S. Senate when he was sworn into office in January 2005. The first major piece of legislation he introduced came two months later with the Higher Education Opportunity through Pell Grant Expansion Act of 2005 (HOPE Act). Its goal was increase the maximum amount that the federal government provides each student who receives need-based financial aid for college. In the 1970s and 1980s, Pell grants often covered nearly the entire tuition cost—excluding room, board, and books—at some state universities. But because they had failed to keep pace with rising tuition costs by 2005 they covered, on average, just 23 percent of the tuition at state schools.

Obama and his wife have two young daughters, Malia and Sasha. Instead of moving to Washington, Michelle Robinson Obama remained in Chicago indefinitely with the children and kept her job as a hospital executive. Television personality Oprah Winfrey (1954–) interviewed Obama not long after the Democratic National Convention and asked him how he became such an eloquent public speaker. He replied that he knew from an early age that he had a career in the persuasive arts—be they legal or political—ahead of him. "I always knew I could express myself," he said in *O, The Oprah Magazine*. "I knew I could win some arguments. I knew I could get my grandparents and mom frustrated!"

For More Information

Books

Obama, Barack. *Dreams from My Father: A Story of Race and Inheritance*. New York: Three Rivers Press, 2004.

Periodicals

Alter, Jonathan. "'The Audacity of Hope.'" *Newsweek* (December 27, 2004): p. 74.

Finnegan, William. "The Candidate." *New Yorker* (May 31, 2004).

Meeks, Kenneth. "Favorite Son." *Black Enterprise* (October 2004): p. 88.

"Oprah Talks to Barack Obama." *O, The Oprah Magazine* (November 2004): p. 248.

Ripley, Amanda. "Obama's Ascent." *Time* (November 15, 2004): p. 74.

Web Sites

Barack Obama, U.S. Senator from Illinois. http://obama.senate.gov/ (accessed on August 23, 2005).

"Rising Star: Senate Candidate Barack Obama Delivers Rousing Keynote at DNC." *Democracy Now.* http://www.democracynow.org/article.pl?sid = 04/07/28/1313225 (accessed on August 23, 2005).

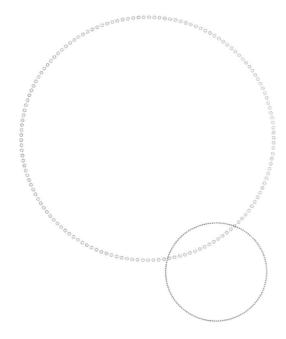

Emeka Okafor

U·X·L newsmakers • *volume 6*

September 28, 1982 • *Houston, Texas*

Basketball player

Emeka Okafor ended his first season with the Charlotte Bobcats, the North Carolina team of the National Basketball Association (NBA), as winner of the league's 2004–05 Rookie of the Year award. A standout athlete during his college career as a center for the University of Connecticut (UConn) Huskies, Okafor was the NBA's second draft pick in 2004. Sportswriters described him as one of the league's future legends, but Okafor also managed to compile an impressive academic record at UConn, graduating with honors and a year early, too.

Father flees Nigeria

Okafor is of Nigerian heritage. He was born Chukwuemeka Noubuisi Okafor in 1982 in Houston, Texas, where his immigrant parents had settled. His father's family had come from the eastern part of Nigeria, a place called Enugwuukwu, but during his father's teen years Nigeria was torn by a civil war that would leave a million dead. A small part of the country had seceded (officially withdrawn) and declared itself independent of Nigeria in 1967, and the newly created republic was called Biafra. The family of Okafor's father wound up in a Biafran refugee camp, where they lived for more than two years. Many there, including Okafor's grandfather, starved or died of illness. Okafor's father, Pius, joined the Biafran army because he knew soldiers were fed before refugees in such crises. Pius managed to survive until the end of the war in 1970, which also marked the end of an independent Biafra. Four years later,

---

"Basketball is a gift, but so is intelligence. I don't want to ever waste either of them."

---

he immigrated to the United States, where one of his cousins had already settled.

After a few months in Louisiana, Okafor's father moved on to Houston, where he worked at a gas station at night while taking classes at Texas Southern University. On a visit home to Nigeria in 1980, he met his future wife, Celestina. After their marriage, she became a nurse, while Pius earned advanced degrees in business and accounting. He worked as an accountant for oil companies in Houston and then Bartlesville, Oklahoma, for a time when Okafor and his younger sister, Nneka, were growing up.

Like his father, Okafor was studious and serious. Once, in the fourth grade, he came home with a "B" on his report card and cried over it. He was also a skilled young athlete, playing soccer and baseball, running track and field events, and swimming competitively. On a playground court near their home, he sharpened his basketball skills with Nneka, who became tired and wanted to go home long before he did. He joined his first basketball team as a sixth-grader. At Houston's Bellaire High School, which attracted some of the city's top students, he played on a freshman squad that won the city championship. Midway through his sophomore year, Bellaire's coaches moved the talented fifteen year old onto the varsity squad as a center and forward for the team.

Emerges as tough shot blocker

Okafor attended a few summer camps for high-school hoops players that are usually sponsored by athletic-shoe companies like Nike. The camps offer teen athletes a chance to improve their game, while scouts for college teams survey the young talent pool. But Okafor was overlooked by college recruiters because he did not have a solid offense style of play at the time. He was, however, an excellent shot blocker, an invaluable resource for any team, preventing the other team from scoring and doing it with a minimum of fouls. Okafor was also tall—by the time he reached his senior year, he stood six feet, nine inches. At that point, he decided he was too thin. He began an impressive weight-training regimen and put twenty pounds on his frame in just six months. College recruiters began to take notice.

Okafor continued to earn nearly straight-A grades at Bellaire. He scored 1310 out of 1600 on his Scholastic Aptitude Test (SAT), placing him among the top-ranked college-bound high-school seniors in the United States, and graduated with a 4.3 grade point average (GPA), out of a possible 4.0; the extra points came from taking advanced placement classes. He hoped to enter Stanford University in California, but its athletic department did not offer him a scholarship. Instead he was courted by Vanderbilt and Rice universities, as well as Georgia Tech.

Okafor chose the University of Connecticut (UConn), mostly because he liked the style of play for which this school and other teams in the Big East Conference were known. Other schools in the athletic conference include Georgetown, Villanova, and Seton Hall universities. Though UConn's main campus at Storrs was known for its rigorous academics, it also had an excellent winning record in college sports, especially basketball. In 1999, the UConn Huskies won the National Collegiate Athletic Association (NCAA) men's basketball championship. The women's basketball team also had winning seasons, taking NCAA titles in 1995 and 2000.

Earns top grades

Okafor arrived at Storrs in the fall of 2001, and he made vast improvements in his game under men's coach Jim Calhoun. He finished his first season as the third best shot blocker in all of college basketball, with a count of 136 shots blocked. He also took eighteen credit hours his first semester, and seventeen credit hours the next. Even during that freshman year, he attracted attention as a possible future NBA star. In March 2002, he was the subject of a *New York Times* article in which sportswriter Joe Drape celebrated Okafor's drive, talent, and ambition—both on the court and off. Okafor admitted that he was as committed to earning good grades as he was to playing for the Huskies. "As much as I love basketball, I want to have options," he explained to Drape in the interview. "I'm goal oriented and I have this thing about failing."

Around this same time, Okafor made his first appearance in the NCAA men's basketball tournament commonly known as "March Madness." The Huskies had racked up a undistinguished 25–6 season record, partly because it was a younger team with Okafor and other freshman and sophomore players. Because of this, they were not expected to do well in the tournament, but went on to beat the Hampton, North Carolina State, and Southern Illinois University (SIU) teams. In that last game, Okafor kept one of SIU's top players, Rolan Roberts (1978–), from scoring for the final seventeen minutes of a game. But Okafor and the UConn team were beaten by the University of Maryland Terrapins, 90–82, who went on to win their first NCAA title in the school's history.

In the 2002–03 season, the Huskies had an even worse win-loss record than the previous year by the time March Madness began. Despite that, they made it into the semifinals after beating Seton Hall, 83–70. From there Okafor and the team defeated

Syracuse University, 80–67, then Stanford University, 85–74, but lost to the University of Texas Longhorns by just four points and exited the tournament.

Leads the Huskies to Final Four

As the 2003–04 basketball season neared, Okafor was anticipating his final year in college—though he was still a junior. He was able to graduate a year ahead of schedule by taking a heavy course load every semester and other tactics. One strategy involved reading a business calculus textbook and then taking the final exam for it, instead of taking the class. This is called "testing out" of required classes, and some top students prefer not to do so, because a poor grade on the exam—which translates into their grade for the class—can lower their GPA. On that business calculus exam, Okafor earned the only "B" on his college record.

Because of his excellent academic record, NCAA leadership liked to point to Okafor as proof that college players could excel in both sports and school. The NCAA rates how well colleges and universities do in balancing athletics and academics, and a school is considered in line with NCAA standards if its athletes graduate within six years. Okafor, in response, has said that the NCAA might do more to help college athletes. Additional game tickets for family members was one way, he said, along with a voucher for the occasional airfare home to visit family. Scholarship money was another issue. "Right now athletes can't keep additional scholarships they earn through academics," he told *Sports Illustrated* journalist Alexander Wolff. "That makes no sense. And the gambling is getting crazy. Every town I go to, some fan is like, 'Emeka, I got a thousand bucks on you guys.' I'm like, 'Great, dude, I don't really care.'"

Becomes NBA draft pick

Okafor's high 3.95 GPA prompted *Basketball Digest* to name him its Player of the Year in December 2003 for excelling on the basketball court as well as in the classroom. He had a tough season, however, due to a stress fracture in his back that caused

During the 2004–05 season, Emeka Okafor led all NBA rookies in scoring, with an average of 15.9 points per game, winning him the NBA Rookie of the Year title. AP/Wide World Photos.

painful spasms, and sportswriters wondered how the Huskies would do in the NCAA tournament if he was benched. He wasn't, and thanks to his impressive performance, UConn advanced to the "Final Four," where the last four teams left in the tournament compete to be in the championship. The UConns won the 2004 NCAA championship after beating Georgia Tech, 82–73. Okafor put in an impressive performance for what would be his final game in college basketball, with 24 points and 15 rebounds. He also won the Most Outstanding Player award at

"A Cat Named Bob"

Emeka Okafor played his rookie season for the Charlotte Bobcats, a National Basketball Association (NBA) franchise in North Carolina's largest city. The Bobcats were also rookies that 2004–05 year, because it was their first season of regular league play as the NBA's newest expansion team. The team is owned by Robert L. Johnson (1946–), the first African American to own a majority stake in an NBA franchise. Born in Mississippi into a family of ten children, Johnson earned a graduate degree from Princeton University in 1972 and was a public-television executive and later vice president of a group of cable-channel owners in the 1970s. In 1979, he founded Black Entertainment Television (BET), a cable channel aimed at African American viewers that went on the air the following year.

Over the next two decades, Johnson expanded BET from a cable channel that aired just two hours of programming daily into an entertainment powerhouse that produced public-affairs programs, gospel events, and even ventured into event promotion with its acclaimed BET Jazz music festival series. In 1999, Viacom bought BET for $2.3 billion in stock. Johnson remained chief executive officer and chair of the cable channel, which reaches sixty-five million homes in the United States, until stepping down in 2005 to devote more time to the Bobcats. He has said that he named

Robert L. Johnson. AP/Wide World Photos.

the team after himself, "a cat named Bob." The rapper Nelly (1978–) owns a minority stake in the Bobcats.

the tournament. Sportswriters predicted he would not play a fourth year with Connecticut and instead turn professional, and on April 16, 2004, Okafor announced that he was giving up his final year of college eligibility to instead declare himself a candidate for the NBA draft.

On June 24, 2004, Okafor was the number two NBA draft pick in the nation, after Dwight Howard, a talented high school player from Georgia who was signed by the Orlando Magic. Okafor was taken by the Charlotte Bobcats, a new NBA expansion team that would be playing its first regular NBA season in 2004–05. He had a good first year in pro basketball under coach Bernie Bickerstaff (1944–), leading the team in points and rebounds. Early in the season, the Bobcats beat the Detroit Pistons, the 2004 NBA champions, and became the first expansion outfit to beat a title-holding team since 1971. Midway through the season, Okafor was named to the NBA All-Star Team. He received 408,082 votes, the most out of any rookie player that year. But the Bobcats did not do as well: with a record of eighteen wins and sixty-four losses, they finished the season in fourth place among the five teams in their Southeastern Division of the Eastern Conference.

During his rookie season, Okafor had nineteen straight double-doubles from mid-November to January. Double-doubles is the statistical term in basketball for game performance numbers that reached double-digits in two of the following categories: points, rebounds, assists, steals, and blocked shots. He also led all NBA rookies in scoring, with an average of 15.9 points per game, and with 10.9 rebounds per game. At the end of the 2004–05 season, he won the NBA Rookie of the Year award, beating out former Huskies teammate Ben Gordon (1983–), who had started his own pro career that year with the Chicago Bulls.

Okafor's teammates teased him when *People* named him "Sexiest NBA Rookie" in its annual issue that ranks celebrity sex appeal. Out of college, he could now devote his spare time to reading for pleasure, and he did a lot of it during travel time to and from away games. "It keeps my mind fresh," he told Chris Ballard in a *Sports Illustrated* interview. "You don't want your brain to rot too badly. You can only watch so many movies and play so many video games."

For More Information

Periodicals

Ballard, Chris."Emeka Okafor: Bobcats Forward." *Sports Illustrated* (April 18, 2005): p. 33.

Drape, Joe. "Okafor Is Quick Study, on Court and in Class." *New York Times* (March 21, 2002): p. C16.

Kertes, Tom. "Center of Attention." *Basketball Digest* (December 003): p. 50.

Kertes, Tom. "The Incomparable Emeka." *Basketball Digest* (July–August 2004): p. 48.

Layden, Tim. "A Student of the Game." *Sports Illustrated* (April 14, 2004): p. 12.

Layden, Tim. "When Brain Meets Brawn." *Sports Illustrated* (November 24, 2003): p. 74.

Wolff, Alexander. "Remember the Alamodome." *Sports Illustrated* (April 14, 2004): p. 46.

Web Sites

Emeka Okafor: 50. http://www.nba.com/playerfile/emeka_okafor/?nav = page (accessed on August 23, 2005).

The Official Site of the Charlotte Bobcats. http://www.nba.com/bobcats/ (accessed on August 23, 2005).

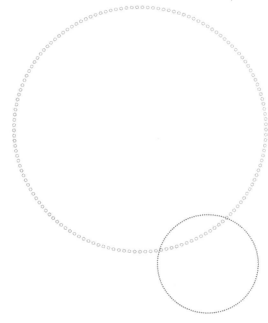

Terrell Owens

December 7, 1973 • *Alexander City, Alabama*

Football player

Terrell Owens is one of the most popular—and controversial—players in the National Football League (NFL). The Alabama native is considered one of the most talented wide receivers in professional football, but has drawn added attention for his battles with his coaches, team executives, and even his fellow players that often play out in the media. In 2004, he was involved in a tense contract dispute with his longtime team, the San Francisco 49ers, over a planned move to the Philadelphia Eagles roster. He has been scorned by sportswriters for what they view as his unsportsmanlike behavior. Those critics, along with "many NFL owners and league executives," Owens wrote in his 2004 autobiography *Catch This!*: "don't know where I came from or what I believe in. They don't want to know too much about the hired hands who make their football machines go. They want us to do our jobs and stay in our places and shut up."

Learns truth about neighbor

In his autobiography, Owens recounts a childhood in which he grew up lonely and poor. He was born Terrell Eldorado Owens on December 7, 1973, to Marilyn Heard, a seventeen year old from Alexander City, Alabama. He was raised primarily by his grandmother in Alex City, as his hometown is known. He wrote about a great-grandmother he never knew in his book. She disappeared one day when his grandmother was twelve years old, and in the pre-civil rights era Deep South, little was done to solve the disappearance. She was simply assumed to have run away, or been murdered. (Before the civil rights movement of

> **"**I'm not going to keep quiet or stay inside a box, the way many pro athletes do, even some very famous ones who've told me that the best road was to be politically correct at all times.**"**

the 1950s and 1960s that pushed for equal rights for all races, blacks suffered severe prejudice and persecution, especially in the former slave states of the South.) The tragedy left a scar on the family that carried over well into Owens's youth. His grandmother was so overly protective of Owens, along with the brother and two sisters of his she also raised, that she did not permit them to leave the front yard to play with other children. Even when Owens received a bike as a gift, he was only allowed to ride it in the driveway or on the sidewalk in front of the house. If the rule was broken, they could expect a whipping. Owens recalls crying as he looked out his bedroom window and watched the other kids play freely on the street.

Owens's mother was not absent from his life, but she had to work double shifts at the nearby Russell Athletic textile mill to support her children, whose fathers did not play a part in their lives. One of the most traumatic events of his early life, Owens wrote in *Catch This!*, was the time he fell in love with the little girl who lived across the street from him. The girl's father—a man in his forties—made fun of the eleven-year-old's crush on his daughter and said dating her was impossible because the girl was Terrell's sister. With this, Owens realized that this neighbor man was his father. He and his family had lived across the street all this time, and neither his grandmother nor his mother, Marilyn Heard, had ever told him about it. He was devastated by the news, and he never went near the house again. Nor did his father make any attempt to have a relationship with him.

Owens and his siblings were allowed to leave the property for two reasons: to go to church and to school. There, kids of his own race teased him because of his darker skin. As a teenager Owens found more acceptance on the football field, and he was a standout player at Benjamin Russell High School as a wide receiver, the member of the offense who can run and catch passes. His hero was San Francisco 49er Jerry Rice (1962–), considered one of, if not the best, wide receivers to ever play in the NFL. Owens even wore Rice's number 80 jersey on his high school team.

Signs with University of Tennessee

Owens was a four-sport athlete at Russell High. He ran track and field, played baseball, and was a talented basketball player as well. He was not even sure that he wanted to devote his energies to football if the chance for an athletic scholarship came—he preferred basketball as his sport of choice instead. Once, he tried to quit the high school football team before his senior year, but the coach convinced him to stay. Owens chose to attend the University of Tennessee (U.T.) at Chattanooga, mostly because the school's athletic director did not object to him playing two sports at the school.

Once again, Owens distinguished himself on the football field with the Mocs, as the U.T. team was called. He set a single-game touchdown record at the school—four in all—in one 1993 game and helped lead the basketball team to the National Collegiate Athletic Association (NCAA) tournament in 1996. That same year, he was a third-round draft pick by the 49ers, taken eighty-ninth overall, and he was thrilled to be joining the team of his longtime idol in the very same position. But his rookie season was a tough year for him, and he didn't get much field time. Few sportswriters thought he would become a strong player on the 49ers roster. That same year, Owens was devastated when his friend from high school, Cedric Kendrick, was killed in car accident back in Alabama.

Owens spent eight seasons with the San Francisco 49ers, but he was a second-string player until Rice was forced out by injury. Owens was eventually teamed with quarterback Jeff Garcia (1970–) and emerged as a strong, if a bit inconsistent, player with game-winning abilities. He could evade defensemen and make amazing catches, and he became known for his antics when he did help the team score. Sometimes he even did a little dance in the end zone, which critics said was a display of unsportsmanlike gloating.

Before the start of the 1999 season, the 49ers signed Owens to a new contract. It was a seven-year, $35 million deal. The team was rewarded the following year when on December 17, 2000, Owens broke an NFL record that had stood for fifty years: in a game against the Chicago Bears, he caught twenty receptions in one game, beating the previous pass-reception single-game record of eighteen set by a Los Angeles Ram player named Tom Fears (1922–2000) on December 3, 1950.

Defends midfield dancing

Earlier that season, Owens had moved beyond dancing in the end zone during a September 2000 game against the Dallas Cowboys at Texas Stadium. After a touchdown, he went out and did a joyous dance on the Cowboys' midfield logo. When he did it a second time, the Dallas crowd erupted in anger. "I was just being creative and having fun," Owens said in his defense in an interview with Thomas George in the *New York Times*. "My intentions were not bad ones. But then, after Emmitt Smith did it after Dallas scored, I felt I had to go back a second time after I scored. The second time I did do it out of spite. But I didn't expect it to create such a stir." Steve Mariucci (1955–), the 49ers respected head coach, suspended Owens for a week and fined him one week's salary as well, which amounted to a $24,294 penalty.

Even behind the scenes, Owens was not the most popular member of the team. Fellow players considered him aloof, and he had some battles with the 49ers coaching staff, too. Once, he told the press that the team had lost to the Chicago Bears because Mariucci was pals with the Bears' coach, Dick Jauron (1950–), and did not give it his best coaching effort that day. On another occasion, Owens criticized Mariucci for the coach's play-calling during one game, claiming that Owens had not been given the ball enough. Mariucci, asked by a reporter about Owens's remarks, called them "devoid of thought" according to Paul Attner in *Sporting News*. The two spent an entire season not speaking more than a minimum of necessary words to one another, but they finally patched things up after Owens met with the 49ers general manager and team owner to talk about it after the 2001 season ended. Two months later, Mariucci flew out to visit Owens at his Atlanta home, where "we just put it all on the table, positive and negative," Owens told *New York Times* sportswriter Damon Hack. "He expressed things he didn't like about me and vice versa. He told me there may have been some things he did wrong—maybe he should have gotten me the ball more—but you live and learn."

Inspires "Sharpie rule"

Owens was involved in another highly publicized incident in October 2002 during a 49ers game against the Seattle Seahawks. When he caught a game-winning touchdown, he took a Sharpie magic marker out of his sock, signed the football, and handed it to his financial advisor, who was sitting in the stands. In response, the NFL issued what became known as the "Sharpie rule," which called for a fifteen-yard penalty or even ejection from the game for any player who takes a foreign object onto the field. All of this controversy did not hinder Owens's performance on the field. He had another career-defining moment during a playoff game against the New York Giants in 2002. He caught 177 yards' worth of receptions and helped the team, which had been losing by 24 points, beat the Giants 39–38.

Despite the talents of Owens and quarterback Jeff Garcia, the 49ers consistently failed to make it to the Super Bowl. It was a source of concern for the team, its owners, and Bay Area fans alike. Owens was not happy about being on a losing team, and he and Garcia did not have a good working relationship, either on the gridiron or off. Owens began dropping hints in the media that he hoped to move on when the 2003 season was over. A clause (part) in his contract gave him the option to become a free agent early in 2004, and that would let him sign with another team. Before that happened, however, the 49ers announced that they had traded Owens to the Baltimore Ravens. An angry Owens told the media he would not play in Baltimore. There was a question of whether he and his sports agent had missed the February 21, 2004, deadline, when he was expected to declare himself a free agent. Owens claimed that in 2001 he had negotiated a March 15 deadline instead and was in contract negotiations with the Eagles when the Ravens trade was announced. The NFL players' association took his side, and a legal battle seemed possible. That was avoided when all parties met at the University of Pennsylvania Law School and a deal was struck: Owens would go to Philadelphia, and Philadelphia would give San Francisco a defensive end player, Brandon Whiting, and also give up its fifth-round 2004 draft-pick slot to Baltimore.

The Eagles signed Owens to a seven-year, $48 million contract, which included a $10 million signing bonus. His number 81 Eagles jersey became the NFL's top-selling piece of merchandise, with sales boosted by his performance during the 2004 season. But controversy still followed him: During a pre-game show for ABC's *Monday Night Football* on November 15, 2004, Owens appeared in a promotional spot with Nicollette Sheridan (1963–), one of the stars of the hit ABC prime-time series *Desperate Housewives*. The skit showed the pair in a locker room, with Sheridan wearing just a towel; she asks Owens to skip the game to be with her and drops the towel to the floor. He says the team will have to do without him, and she jumps into his arms. The promotional spot was produced by ABC Sports, and it prompted a flood of angry phone calls and letters to the network, for it had aired at a time when many under-age viewers were watching. There was even a formal inquiry by the Federal Communications Commission (FCC), the government

Owens v. McNabb

Terrell Owens and Philadelphia Eagles quarterback Donovan McNabb (1976–) were predicted to become an unbeatable combination as Philadelphia fans anticipated Owens's first season with the team in 2004. The expectations were satisfied with a record-setting season, and one in which McNabb finally emerged as a star quarterback after five somewhat undistinguished years with the team.

The Eagles started the 2004 season with an astonishing seven-game winning streak. They became the division's first-place champs when there were still five weeks of games left to play. In NFL history, only two other teams ever achieved a first-place finish that early. In all, McNabb threw thirty-one touchdowns, and Owens caught fourteen of them. This helped McNabb end the regular season with statistics that made him the NFL's fourth-ranked quarterback. "Owens has given the Eagles a dimension they had lacked," noted sports broadcaster and former Dallas Cowboys quarterback Troy Aikman in *Sporting News* in early October. "He's not a great route runner and doesn't have the best hands, but he's fast, he's big and physical, and he's deadly after the catch. McNabb has never had a weapon like Owens before."

The Eagles went on to Super Bowl XXXIX, but lost to the New England Patriots. A few months later, Owens—with what his critics said was his characteristic verbal recklessness—made some comments to the media that seemed to question McNabb's performance. "I wasn't the guy who got tired in the Super Bowl," he told ESPN.com, according to a *Houston Chronicle* article by John McClain. There

Donovan McNabb. © Shaun Best/Reuters/Corbis.

were reports that McNabb was winded and ill in the final quarter after being hit too hard earlier in the game. "I wasn't tired, (but) I'm not going to sit here and try to have a war of words," McNabb said in response. In mid-August, that war heated up when Owens called McNabb a "hypocrite" on ESPN because of an earlier media report in which the quarterback said he had no desire to meet with Owens to patch up their differences.

agency charged with regulating the airwaves. ABC Sports was attacked for the spot, which seemed to be using sex to promote professional sports, but Owens was also criticized for participating in it. He issued a public apology, as did the NFL.

Makes Super Bowl debut

A month later, Owens sprained his ankle and fractured a fibula, one of the bones in his calf, in a game against the Dallas Cowboys. The Eagles said he would likely be out the rest of the season, but Owens contradicted that and said he would play in the coming Super Bowl, when the Eagles would meet the New England Patriots. He underwent leg surgery and played well during Super Bowl XXXIX, with nine receptions. The Eagles lost, however, 24–21. Later, Owens made negative remarks about Eagles quarterback Donovan McNabb, and he announced he had a new agent—the aggressive and controversial Drew Rosenhaus—and wanted to renegotiate his Eagles contract. As summer neared, he asked Eagles management to let him play on a summer-league squad of the Sacramento Kings of the National Basketball Association, but they refused. At one point, he even hinted that he might not show up for the official start of training camp, but in July said he would return to the Eagles roster for the 2005 season. He did appear, but in characteristic form was suspended for a week for disrespectful behavior. He then began appearing with his agent on talk shows, during which he made negative comments about his coach, Andy Reid, and his fellow players.

Owens has a son, Terique, who was born in 1999. He has contributed his time and celebrity to the Alzheimer Foundation and has spoken publicly on several occasions about his grandmother's diagnosis with the debilitating condition that deteriorates the memory and other mental activity. In his autobiography, he wrote about the troubles he has had with authority figures and teammates over the years, but says that a deep spiritual strength has helped him grow. "My grandmother and my mom taught me that I need to walk through this world with a strong mind and a big heart, so that's my goal," he wrote. "I don't always reach it. Sometimes I stumble, and sometimes I come close to falling, but then I refocus and try to learn and get better."

For More Information

Books

Owens, Terrell, and Stephen Singular. *Catch This!: Going Deep with the NFL's Sharpest Weapon.* New York: Simon & Schuster, 2004.

Periodicals

Aikman, Troy. "A Chemistry Lesson in Philly." *Sporting News* (October 18, 2004): p. 71.

Attner, Paul. "Get Used T.O. It." *Sporting News* (October 28, 2002): p. 20.

Attner, Paul. "Turned on but Still Ticked Off." *Sporting News* (June 14, 2004): p. 28.

Brookover, Bob. "Owens Wants to Play in NBA, but Expect Eagles to Say No." *Philadelphia Inquirer* (July 1, 2005).

"Dungy Calls 'Monday Night' Sketch Racially Insensitive." *New York Times* (November 18, 2004): p. D4.

George, Thomas. "Getting Wish, Owens to Join the Eagles." *New York Times* (March 17, 2004): p. D1.

George, Thomas. "Here Comes Terrell Owens; The 49ers Have a Receiver Who Can No Longer Be Ignored." *New York Times* (January 13, 2002): p. SP2.

Hack, Damon. "The 49ers' Uneasy Truce; Coach and Star Receiver Reach Out to Each Other." *New York Times* (September 4, 2002): p. A25.

Hirshberg, Charles. "Sympathy for the Showboat (Book Review)." *Sports Illustrated* (November 15, 2004): p. Z12.

Longman, Jere. "Eagles Are Preparing for Life without Owens." *New York Times* (July 5, 2005): p. C5.

McClain, John. "Owens' Verbal Jabs Miff McNabb." *Houston Chronicle* (May 1, 2005): p. 18.

"Owens Looks to Be the Family Rock." *San Francisco Examiner* (August 13, 2000).

"Question and Answer with Terrell Owens. " *Philadelphia Inquirer* (March 9, 2004).

Rhoden, William C. "In 'Monday Night' Fallout, a Deeper Racial Issue." *New York Times* (November 21, 2004): p. SP11.

Web Sites

 # 81 Terrell Owens. http://sports.espn.go.com/nfl/players/profile?statsId = 3664 (accessed on August 23, 2005).

"McNabb Said He Isn't Bothered by T.O.'S Talk." *ESPN.com.* http://sports.espn.go.com/nfl/news/story?id = 2132446 (accessed on August 23, 2005).

The Official Web Site of Terrell Owens. http://terrellowens.com (accessed on September 22, 2005).

Zac Posen

October 24, 1980 • New York, New York

Fashion designer

American designer Zac Posen emerged as fashion's newest star in 2002 when his alluringly feminine dresses made their New York City runway debut. Though he was still rather young to be a business owner, Posen earned enthusiastic write-ups on the pages of *Vogue* and other esteemed fashion magazines for his creative flair. He was hailed as the design world's latest prodigy, and possibly even the savior who might rescue American fashion from the styles-and-sales slump it had experienced over the past decade. *New York Times* writer Guy Trebay was an early champion of Posen, noting in a September 2002 article that the twenty-two-year-old designer "occupies an important symbolic position in the fashion system one hears so much about. He is the future."

Raised in lively New York City neighborhood

Posen is a native New Yorker, and his rapid rise in fashion was partly fueled by personal connections to some well-known tastemakers in the worlds of art and film. His father, Stephen Posen, was a painter, and his mother, Susan, was an attorney who worked in corporate finance. Born in October 1980, he and his older sister grew up in a loft home in the midst of SoHo, an area of lower Manhattan that takes its name from its location "south of Houston" Street. The small factories that had flourished in SoHo

> **"I don't have a formula, except that I don't believe in playing it safe."**

since the nineteenth century moved out, and beginning in the 1960s artists and daring New Yorkers in search of large living spaces began converting the industrial buildings to residential use. By the time Posen was a small child, SoHo had hit its peak of gritty, downtown New York urban cool, and it was humming with art galleries, boutiques, and upscale restaurants.

Posen was a creative child. For his toy figures he made outfits out of unusual materials, like seaweed, and staged puppet shows for his family. "I used to steal yarmulkes [a Jewish head covering traditionally restricted to males] so that I could make bell dresses for dolls," he told *People* writer Michelle Tauber about his visits to Jewish religious services with his family. But Posen also noted that while his parents were extremely supportive of his childhood interests and hobbies, at times he was a bit uneasy with them himself. His interest in fashion "was definitely something, when you're a boy, that you're ashamed of," he admitted in the same interview.

Posen attended St. Ann's School in Brooklyn Heights, a private school that combined academics with a focus on the creative arts. As a teen, he was known for the sometimes outlandish outfits he wore to school, some of them bought off thrift store racks but embellished at home on his sewing machine. A pair of trousers with antlers attached to them was one of his more memorable ensembles. One schoolmate at St. Ann's was Lola Schnabel, daughter of painter Julian Schnabel, a well-known figure in the New York art world of the 1980s. The two became close friends, and their bond was cemented by the fact that both suffered from dyslexia, a reading difficulty.

Makes dresses for teen pals

Posen excelled in math but was drawn to the visual arts. He designed costumes for school plays at St. Ann's and continued to create unusual outfits. He landed his first design commission at the age of fifteen, when Lola Schnabel's little sister, Stella, then twelve, asked him to make a dress for her to wear to an event. She told him she wanted to appear as if she was without clothing, and so Posen created a skin-colored gown from velvet that caused a stir when Schnabel was photographed at the event.

Around 1996 Posen landed a much-coveted internship at the Costume Institute of the Metropolitan Museum of Art in New York City, and there he was able to closely examine the work of masterful fashion designers of the past, such as Madeleine Vionnet (1876–1975), a French pioneer who cut her dresses on the bias, a method that highlighted a woman's curves and eliminated unnecessary details. He also took courses at the Parsons School of Design in the city in its pre-college summer program, and landed another impressive internship, this one with designer Nicole Miller (1952–) in 1998. The first piece he drew at Miller's studio was for a white shirt made out of poplin (a tightly woven cotton material), which was selected to go into production. A year later, he took a job as a design assistant with Tocca, a hot new label.

Though Posen had been accepted into an Ivy League school, Brown University in Rhode Island, he chose to move to London instead to enroll in a highly regarded art school, Central St. Martin's College of Art and Design. Hoping to impress the associate who called him in for an entrance interview, he showed up with ivy trailing from his long, curly hair, and won a spot in its fashion and textiles program. The school, like St. Ann's, was known for its freewheeling atmosphere, but Central St. Martin's also placed immense importance on finding one's creative vision through independent work habits. Not surprisingly, Posen flourished there. He admitted, however, that the decision to attend an art college had not been met with overwhelming enthusiasm back at home. "My parents were always very supportive of anything I was interested in," he explained in an interview with Kathryn Wexler of the *Miami Herald,* but admitted that with his decision to enroll at a "fashion school for college, it became more of a question. My mom and grandparents value a liberal arts education."

Review in the *New York Times*

To help pay living expenses in London, Posen started a private couture, or custom-made clothing business, which grew by word of mouth. That changed in February 2001, when a dress that he made was actually the subject of an article in the "Fashions of the Times" supplement of the *New York Times Magazine*. The dress first had been spotted in December 2000 by journalist Daisy Garnett at a private party in Greenwich Village in New York City. It was worn by a sixteen-year-old woman, Paz de la Huerta, an actor who had been escorted to the party by Posen. "It was dark pink," Garnett wrote, "made of brushed silk, and it tied up in a knot at the back.... It looked like it had been found in a trunk belonging to a 1930's Parisian dancing girl who had been inspired by the paintings of [French Post-Impressionist painter] Toulouse-Lautrec and created a dream dress for kicking up her heels in Montmartre."

Posen had originally made the dress for model Naomi Campbell (1970–), who was a friend of Lola Schnabel's. In the February newspaper article, Garnett wrote that the dress had been borrowed by actor Jade Malle for the January 2001 wedding of Kate Hudson (1979–) and rock singer Chris Robinson (1966–). Malle knew Posen through her cousin, who had attended St. Ann's; Malle had once borrowed a halter dress that Posen had made for her cousin, "and as I walked down the street, strangers stopped and begged me to tell them where I got this dress," Malle

The Posen-Portman Connection

American designer Zac Posen owes much of his early success to having some of his first dresses worn by glamorous young film stars, including Claire Danes (1979–) and Natalie Portman (1981–). Portman's entrance at the London premier of *Star Wars: Episode II—Attack of the Clones* in May 2002 helped boost his career immensely. Posen has referred to Portman as his muse, or inspiration, following a fashion tradition of designer-actress alliances, such as Narcisso Rodriguez and Sarah Jessica Parker (1965–), and Marc Jacobs and Sofia Coppola (1971–). Jacobs even named a handbag in honor of the Academy Award-winning director of *Lost in Translation.*

Posen and Portman have often been photographed together at high-profile events, such as the 2002 VH1 Fashion Awards. "Zac's clothes are classical and elegant but also made for young people," Portman told *People.*

told Garnett. "The Fashions of the Times" article generated major buzz for Posen, as did a leather dress that was featured in a Central St. Martin's exhibition of Victorian undergarments. The complex frock, made of lengthy strips of glossy leather held together by hundreds of hook-and-eye closures was also chosen to appear in London's Victoria and Albert Museum, and it eventually became part of that museum's permanent collection.

Despite his success, Posen was forced to return to New York, as he told the *Miami Herald.* "I couldn't legally work in London, and I couldn't afford to live there," he said. Moving back into his parents' home, he opened a small space above a New York boutique, and by late 2001 had established his own label, as well as a company he called Outspoke, which was managed by his mother. In December a line of his dresses began selling at the posh Manhattan retailer Henri Bendel.

First collection earns terrific praise

Posen's first real runway show came in February 2002, and he staged it at a former synagogue in New York's once-neglected Bowery neighborhood on the Lower East Side. In the audience

Actress Natalie Portman brought attention to Zac Posen's work by being one of the first big celebrities to wear his designs. © Petre Buzoianu/Corbis.

that day was Barbara Bush, daughter of U.S. president George W. Bush (1946–), along with the woman considered the most powerful in fashion, American *Vogue* editor Anna Wintour (1949–). Though such runway presentations are costly to mount, Posen used the prize money he received from winemaker Ecco Domani and its Foundation Award for Young Designers. The rest came from private contributions from his family and friends. It was a well-chronicled event in the fashion press and earned Posen several enthusiastic reviews as well as many new clients.

Posen's next show was held in September 2002 during New York Fashion Week, when store buyers and journalists are offered a glimpse of the next season's designer lines. It coincided with a tremendous honor for such a young designer: his dresses had recently gone on sale at Bloomingdale's, and the department store's flagship New York emporium had devoted an entire row of windows to Posen's line. The dresses were priced in the $1,200 to $1,500 range, and *Time* journalist Belinda Luscombe found them "1940s-style shapely; they flare at the hem and enhance the bust and waist. Several spring looks are constructed of thin bands of material sewn together horizontally, like belts, that can be adjusted."

Posen's star continued to rise over the next few years. He showed his collections at the twice-yearly New York Fashion Week, and his dresses became a favorite of the fashionista set, the passel of stylish and influential women who work in fashion, either at design houses or in journalism and public relations. He was not immune to the lures of his dresses himself. "I like to try on my clothing and see how it feels," he told Tauber in *People*. "That's really important—to see how something makes you feel."

Strikes a deal with Diddy

Posen's Fall 2004 collection, staged during New York Fashion Week earlier that same year, featured his first foray into sportswear. The collection's theme was "Blixen," named in part after the writer Karen Blixen (1885–1962), the Danish baroness born Isak Dinesen who penned the novel *Out of Africa*. The term "Blixen" also touched upon two other meanings: the German word for lightning, and the name of one of Santa's reindeer. "Not only was this his most accomplished collection to date, it was also one of the best of the fall season," remarked *New York Times* fashion writer Cathy Horyn, who liked the juxtaposition of fabrics and colors. "The clothes had much going for them: youth, wit, technical finesse but, above all, real sophistication," Horyn asserted.

Yet Horyn also wrote another article about Posen's impressive rise in the cutthroat fashion world that appeared just eight days later in the *New York Times* that contained a few disapproving comments. "Success in fashion is one part talent, one part luck and one part a tireless ability to hold a gaudy marquee over your head," Horyn wrote. "Posen has all these qualities in excess." Nevertheless, Horyn conceded that "I have also come to the conclusion that of all the young designers gathering on the horizon, Posen is the one who is most likely to break through precisely because he possesses all the same qualities that worked so beautifully for his predecessors in this venal [capable of being corrupted] industry."

Posen teamed with rap impresario Sean "Diddy" Combs (1969–) in the spring of 2004 for a business venture. Combs, a producer and record-label mogul with his own clothing line called Sean John, made an undisclosed financial investment in Posen's company. Business writers and fashion industry analysts viewed it as a smart move that would help take Posen's company to another level thanks to the mass retail connections that Sean Jean Clothing had already forged in the industry.

Despite the deal, Posen was determined to maintain a close-knit corporate inner circle staffed by friends and family. His mother serves as chief executive officer of Outspoke and vice chair of the venture with Combs's company. His older sister, Alexandra, is his creative director, and a grown-up Stella Schnabel is his stylist. "I love the industry," Posen told Marc Jacobs (1963–) when he and the older American designer— to whom Posen has often been compared—interviewed one another for a June 2003 issue of *WWD*. "It's amazing and overwhelming." Posen offered up a piece of advice to aspiring designers or creative types: "I think one should follow their dreams and should always persevere." "Something that's been really important to me is to physically make your clothing and put it on as many different kinds of people as you can to see how they feel in it. And find your vision and put it out there."

For More Information

Periodicals

"Breakthroughs 2002." *People* (December 30, 2002): p. 134.

Garnett, Daisy. "A Star Is Born." *New York Times* ("Fashions of the Times") (February 25, 2001): p. 66.

Horyn, Cathy. "A Little Bit Adorable." *New York Times Magazine* (February 22, 2004): p. 66.

Horyn, Cathy. "Sophistication of the Slinky Sort." *New York Times* (February 14, 2004): p. B6.

Huckbody, Jamie. "The Man Who Would Be King." *Independent* (London, England) (February 14, 2003): p. 6.

Kato, Donna. "Distinctive Style, Business Savvy Make Fashion Designer Zac Posen Star at 24." *San Jose Mercury News* (December 19, 2004).

Luscombe, Belinda. "Boy in Vogue." *Time* (September 30, 2002): p. 78.

"Marc and Zac." *WWD* (June 2, 2003): p. 36S.

Rubenstein, Hal. "The Look of Zac Posen (Fashion/The Look)." *In Style* (December 1, 2003): p. 152.

Tauber, Michelle. "Sew Cool." *People* (September 15, 2003): p. 153.

Trebay, Guy. "At 21, a Grasp of Women's Clout." *New York Times* (February 12, 2002): p. B8.

Trebay, Guy. "The Rise and Rise of a Prodigy." *New York Times* (September 18, 2002): p. B9.

Wexler, Kathryn. "Boy Wonder: Designer Zac Posen Set Fashion World on Fire at 20." *Miami Herald* (May 4, 2004).

Wilson, Eric, and Julee Greenberg. "Combs Hopes to Score Hit with Posen." *WWD* (April 21, 2004): p. 3.

Web Sites

Zac Posen Official Web Site. http://www.zacposen.com (accessed on August 23, 2005).

Dan Rather

October 31, 1931 • *Wharton, Texas*

Television journalist

Veteran Columbia Broadcasting System (CBS) news anchor Dan Rather retired in 2005 after twenty-four years at the desk of the television network's nightly newscast *CBS Evening News.* Long known in the industry for his aggressive reporting and folksy sayings, Rather is one of the most famous television news journalists of the twentieth century. When he retired, he was the longest-serving anchor on a nightly network newscast in American broadcast history.

Born in rural Texas

Rather was born on October 31, 1931, and was the first of three children in his family. His mother was named Veda, and his father, Daniel Irvin Rather, laid pipeline for Texas oil fields. The family moved to Houston about a year after Rather was born and settled into a working-class neighborhood there. Rather has said that his father was devoted to two things: reading the daily newspapers, and his employer, Humble Oil. He would not buy gas, for example, at any filling station that was not part of the company network.

As a child, Rather's interest in journalism was sparked by a bout of rheumatic fever, an inflammatory reaction that affects the heart, that came on when he was ten years old. He was forced to spend weeks resting in bed, and so he listened to the radio to pass the time. The broadcasts he loved best were the reports delivered by pioneering American war correspondents such as Eric Sevareid (1912–1992) and Edward R. Murrow (1908–1965).

"Rather is the last of his breed, a junkyard dog in anchor's clothing, hard-charging and afraid of nothing except maybe getting caught behind the desk while the town is burning."

Reporter Gary Cartwright in *Texas Monthly*

They were filing radio news stories from European capitals and battlefields during World War II (1939–45; war in which Great Britain, France, the United States, and their allies defeated Germany, Italy, and Japan). By the time he reached his teen years, Rather had decided to become a journalist, though his goal was to work for a major daily newspaper, not a radio network.

Rather entered Sam Houston State Teachers College in Huntsville, Texas, and in 1953 became the first member of his family to earn a college degree. He majored in journalism, but the college's program was not a strong one in that subject, and so he took a series of jobs while still in school that gave him hands-on experience. He worked part time at a Huntsville radio station and then worked as a reporter for the Associated Press wire service; later, he moved on to its competitor, United Press International (UPI). He also served as editor of the campus newspaper.

Rather served a brief stint in the U.S. Marine Corps, but when his superior officers learned about his childhood bout with rheumatic fever, he was disqualified for military service for health reasons. In 1954, he went to work at the *Houston Chronicle*—but not at the paper itself, which had been his longtime career goal. Instead he worked at a radio station owned by the newspaper, KTRH. "I came in at four in the morning," Rather recalled in an interview with Gary Cartwright for *Texas Monthly,* "and read the pork belly futures out of Chicago," or the Chicago Mercantile Exchange trading price for the bacon-providing part of a hog. Eager to prove himself, he persuaded his boss to give him his own show during an open time slot on Sunday, which had been his only day off.

Earns nickname "Hurricane Dan"

Rather tried to land a job at the *Houston Chronicle* newspaper, but he was a poor speller—print journalists of the era needed to be able to write quickly with few errors. His on-air talents were noticed by his station bosses, however, and he was made KTRH's news director in 1956. Three years later, he moved on to the relatively new medium of television as a reporter for KTRK-TV, also in Houston. In January 1960, he became news director for another Houston television station, KHOU, which was an affiliate of CBS. By this time he had married Jean Goebel, whom he met when she was hired as a secretary at KTRH, and they had two small children.

Rather's career moved to a national level thanks to a terrible tropical storm. In September 1961, Hurricane Carla headed toward the American coastline along the Gulf of Mexico. It hit at full force near Galveston, Texas, and became one of the worst storms ever to reach the U.S. mainland. Rather and his team were the only live television news source broadcasting from Galveston when Carla hit, and he delivered one of his reports by hanging onto a palm tree. Rather also persuaded the director of the local weather-reporting station to let his crew put a television camera in front of the radar screen, which tracked storms from high above Earth's atmosphere. "That day," noted Cartwright, "viewers saw something they had never seen

"What's the frequency, Kenneth?"

Veteran CBS anchor Dan Rather was a victim of one of the strangest celebrity-stalking incidents of the modern age. One night in October 1986, he was returning from dinner at a friend's house and walking along Park Avenue in a relatively high-class part of New York City. He was approached by two men, one of whom punched him in the jaw; when Rather ran off, he was chased into a building and kicked. His attacker repeatedly asked him, "Kenneth, what is the frequency?" The assailant, or pair of assailants, ran off. The odd incident inspired a song by alternative rock group R.E.M., "What's the Frequency, Kenneth?," and Rather even joined the band once on stage and sang it with lead singer Michael Stipe.

In 1997, a man in prison for the 1994 murder of an NBC stagehand outside the *Today Show* told his prison psychiatrist that he had attacked Rather back in 1986. Shown photographs of the prisoner, Rather identified William Tager as his attacker. Tager had believed that the news media were trying to send him coded messages, and the matter seemed to rest with that confession.

In 2001, *Harper's* magazine published a piece by Paul Allman that posed several semi-comical questions about the "Kenneth" incident. Allman pointed out that the writer Donald Barthelme (1931–), sometimes called the father of postmodern literary American fiction, had once written a short story containing the phrase "What's the frequency?" as well as the name "Kenneth." In another story of Barthelme's, there is an arrogant "editor-king" named Mr. Lather. Allman's article, and a subsequent stage play produced in New York City, hinted that Barthelme possibly may have been connected to the attack. Allman pointed out that both Barthelme and Rather were Texas natives, born just six months apart, and both had worked in Houston early in their careers—Barthelme as a reporter for the *Houston Post*, while Rather was a radio newsperson. "Is it possible that they could not have known each other, or of each other, in the Houston of the late 1950s and early 1960s?" Allman wondered. "That they could not have attended the same journalistic functions? Or that Rather, the rising star, could not have been the object of envy and speculation on the part of his peers?"

on live television: the image of a four-hundred-mile-wide hurricane superimposed over a map of the Texas Gulf Coast. The coverage spurred a mass evacuation of the coast and probably saved thousands of lives."

Rather's fearless reporting earned the attention of CBS executives in New York City and forever earned him the nickname "Hurricane Dan" among his professional colleagues in the media. Shortly after Hurricane Carla, he was promoted to serve as the network's national news correspondent for its southwestern bureau, which included several southern U.S. states as well as Mexico and Central America. On November 22, 1963, President John F. Kennedy (1917–1963; served 1961–63) was assassinated in his presidential motorcade in Dallas, and Rather once again became the frontperson for CBS coverage on the scene. Within months, he was promoted again, this time to White House correspondent for CBS in Washington, D.C.

Critics call him biased

As a national news reporter, Rather went on to cover some of the most important news stories of the era, including the Vietnam War (1954–75; a controversial war in which the United States aided South Vietnam in its fight against a takeover by Communist North Vietnam) and the series of scandals known as Watergate, which forced the resignation of two-term Republican president Richard M. Nixon (1913–1994; served 1969–74). Rather's aggressive coverage of the Watergate story brought some criticism. He was condemned by Nixon supporters for what they viewed as his liberal bias, or favoritism toward Democratic politics. The unofficial code of ethics for journalists calls for them to remain neutral in their news reporting.

Rather had an infamous exchange with Nixon that caused hundreds of viewers to call or write CBS headquarters in New York City and demand that the network fire him. At a National Association of Broadcasters convention in Houston in March 1974, Nixon was part of one day's program of events. Rather rose to ask the president a question, and some other journalists began booing Rather—but others quickly responded with applause. Taken by surprise at the outburst, Nixon asked Rather, "Are you running for something?" according to Ken Auletta in the *New Yorker*. Rather's response, as quoted by Auletta, was "No, sir, Mr. President. Are you?" The remark was viewed by some as disrespectful, and there were rumors that CBS executives were indeed thinking about firing him for such a daring breach of press–presidential etiquette.

Instead, Rather was taken off the White House beat, and he spent a few years producing documentaries for the network in New York City; he also anchored the *CBS Weekend News*. In 1975, he became a correspondent on the highly rated newsmagazine *60 Minutes*. When veteran CBS news journalist Walter

Cronkite (1916–) announced that he would retire as the anchor of CBS's flagship broadcast, the *CBS Evening News,* Rather was named his successor. It was a tremendous accomplishment, for Cronkite was a giant among broadcast journalists of his era and regularly cited in U.S. public opinion polls as the most trusted person in television news. Rather made his debut on the *CBS Weekend News* on March 9, 1981, and retired exactly twenty-four years later. His tenure made him the longest-serving anchor of a nightly national newscast in U.S. media history.

But Rather was not always at the desk. Again, he took his camera crews to the field and reported from around the world to cover breaking stories and planned events, too. In September 1987, he was in Miami to cover the visit of Pope John Paul II (1920–2005) to that city, but that day his broadcast was to follow CBS Sports's coverage of the U.S. Open tennis match. When one of the games ran into overtime, the network decided to keep it on the air and not switch over to the *CBS Evening News.* Angered, Rather walked off the set to call his boss, the president of CBS News, but then the match ended unexpectedly just two minutes into the hour, and Rather was missing when the cameras began rolling. He was gone for over six minutes in what is known in live radio and television broadcasting as "dead air."

Angers vice president

Rather was again criticized for his behavior, and even other journalists called him unprofessional. The incident returned to the headlines several months later, when Rather was interviewing George H.W. Bush (1924–), who was serving as Republican vice president under Ronald Reagan (1911–2004; served 1981–89). At the time, the Reagan White House was involved in a political scandal known as the Iran-Contra affair, in which some members of the administration were linked to the illegal sale of arms to Iran, an enemy of the United States, in order to finance secret operations in Central America. On the air, Rather questioned Bush relentlessly, as was his style, and the exchange became heated. Finally, according to the *New Yorker,* the vice president responded, "It's not fair to judge my whole career by a rehash

Dan Rather delivered his final broadcast in March 2005, just one year shy of his twenty-fifth anniversary as the **CBS Evening News** *anchorman.* AP/Wide World Photos.

on Iran. How would you like it if I judged your career by those seven minutes when you walked off the set?"

Once again, Rather was accused of showing disrespect to the highest elected officials in the nation, and particularly to Republicans. His daily newscasts were even monitored on a Web site, RatherBiased.com, which tracked the news anchor's alleged lack of impartiality. "I do have my biases," Rather joked in an interview with Auletta in the *New Yorker,* "such as, I'm hard to herd and impossible to stampede," meaning he won't follow the crowd or be pushed over.

That stubbornness was widely suspected of spurring Rather's somewhat unexpected decision to retire from *CBS Evening News,* which was announced in November 2004. Two months earlier, Rather delivered a report on *60 Minutes II* that was based on a series of recently uncovered documents related to

George W. Bush's (1946–) service in the Texas Air National Guard between 1968 and 1973. One of the documents was a memo that seemed to confirm rumors that a young Bush had received special treatment thanks to his family connections. During the Vietnam War era, there was a draft that required young men to register for possible military service; one way to avoid being sent to fight overseas was to serve instead at home in a National Guard unit, which generally required a weekend of service each month at a training camp in one's home state. Rather's report about Bush's record, which seemed to show that the future president often failed to report for Guard duty, was a major journalistic triumph. Most of the major U.S. news organizations had long tried to find documents that would prove the rumors true about Bush's record. Almost immediately, however, the authenticity of the documents was questioned.

Blames "partisan political operatives"

Rather called on Bush to answer the lingering questions about his military service, and he mentioned on *CBS Evening News* that "partisan political operatives" seemed to be behind the controversy over his report, according to a *New York Observer* article by Joe Hagan. In an interview with Hagan, Rather defended his *60 Minutes II* staff who had put together the story, and he pointed out that the debate seemed rather fishy. "If you can't deny the information," he theorized in the interview, "then attack and seek to destroy the credibility of the messenger, the bearer of the information." Rather stood by the report and his staff, but CBS called for an independent investigation into the matter. In the end, four members of the *60 Minutes II* team, including Rather's longtime producer, lost their jobs.

In November 2004, not long after the independent review panel was summoned, Rather announced his decision to retire from the *CBS Evening News*. His last broadcast came in March 2005, a full year ahead of his twenty-fifth anniversary, which he had often said would be his retirement date. Some media analysts and critics of Rather's claimed the National Guard story was the real reason behind the decision, and more moderate voices noted that the rush to get the story on the air without first verifying the authenticity of the documents was merely a sign of the decline of network news. Others called it a triumph of amateur blog (Web log) journalists, who had rushed to post stories questioning the authenticity of the documents while the *60 Minutes II* broadcast was still on the air.

Though Rather officially retired from the *CBS Evening News* anchor desk, he continued to serve as a *60 Minutes II* correspondent. Just before his final broadcast, after twenty-four years on the air, Rather reflected on his long career as CBS's leading newsperson. "My hope has always been, for all my flaws and weaknesses," he told Cartwright in *Texas Monthly,* "that people will say this: 'He wanted to be a reporter and he is.' I think they know that I love this country."

For More Information

Periodicals

Allman, Paul Limbert. "The Frequency: Solving the Riddle of the Dan Rather Beating." *Harper's* (December 2001): p. 69.

Auletta, Ken. "Sign-Off." *New Yorker* (March 7, 2005): p. 48.

Cartwright, Gary. "Dan Rather Retorting." *Texas Monthly* (March 2005): p. 136.

Gay, Jason. "Hurricane Dan's Last Stand." *New York Observer* (May 14, 2001): p. 1.

Hagan, Joe. "Dan Rather to Bush: 'Answer the Questions.'" *New York Observer* (September 20, 2004): p. 1.

Morrow, Lance. "In the Kingdom of Television." *Time* (February 8, 1988): p. 27.

"Rather Identifies Man He Said Beat Him in '86." *San Francisco Chronicle* (January 30, 1997): p. A3.

Zinoman, Jason. "Socking It to Dan Rather: A Nonpolitical Whodunit." *New York Times* (October 29, 2004): p. E2.

Web Sites

CBS Evening News: Dan Rather. http://www.cbsnews.com/stories/2002/02/25/eveningnews/main502026.shtml (accessed on August 23, 2005).

RatherBiased.com: Documenting America's Most Politicized Journalist. http://www.ratherbiased.com (accessed on September 25, 2005).

Rilo Kiley

Rock band

The Los Angeles-based alternative-rock band Rilo Kiley cemented their reputation as a favorite among rock critics with the release of their 2004 album *More Adventurous*. Fronted by Jenny Lewis, a former child actor, the band's introspective, musically complex songs won them a cult following early on in their career in the late 1990s, but the release of *More Adventurous,* their third record, on the Warner label gave them access to a much wider audience. Their songs have even appeared on the hit Fox teen drama *The O.C.*

Settled in southern California

Rilo Kiley was formed when Lewis met guitarist/songwriter Blake Sennett in the mid-1990s. Born on January 8, 1977, Lewis shares a birthday with rock and roll icons David Bowie (1947–) and Elvis Presley (1935–1977). Show-business roots run deep in her family, on her mother's side. "My grandparents were in vaudeville," she told *Times* of London journalist Steve Jelbert, while "my parents had a lounge act in Las Vegas." Her parents' act was similar to that of Sonny (Bono; 1935–1998) and Cher (1946–), husband-and-wife musical stars of their own early 1970s television series. And Lewis's parents, like Sonny and Cher, split up, both professionally and personally.

Lewis had already made her professional debut as a three year old, when she was cast in a television commercial for Jell-O. After her parents divorced when she was around eight years old, Lewis moved from Las Vegas with her mother to southern

> "You can still remain loyal to an indie spirit, but if you hope to reach more people, working with a major label is something to consider.... If we hadn't done it, we probably would have regretted it more."
>
> **Jenny Lewis, lead singer of Rilo Kiley**

California and began working as a child actor. She appeared in television and film projects that included *Life with Lucy,* a short-lived 1986 television series in which she played the sitcom grand-daughter of legendary comedienne Lucille Ball (1911–1989), and *Foxfire,* a 1996 teenage-girl vigilante flick that also starred a young Angelina Jolie (1975–). "Acting was my mother's idea," Lewis explained in an interview with Robert Sandall for London's *Daily Telegraph.* "It was what I did to support the family."

Lewis began writing songs in her teens, inspired in part by her mother's vast record collection heavy on female singer-songwriters, such as Bette Midler (1945–) and Barbra Streisand (1942–). Meeting Sennett was a turning point in her life when the two were introduced by a mutual friend, she told the

Frontperson Jenny Lewis at a 2005 Rilo Kiley performance in California. Tim Mosenfelder/Getty Images.

Philadelphia Inquirer's Dan DeLuca. "Up until then it seemed really far-fetched that anyone would be interested in anything I had to say," she remarked in the interview. Sennett, who grew up in San Diego, had some musical experience as a drummer for a Goth band in his teens, but he had also been a child television actor. He was a regular on *Boy Meets World* from 1994 to 1996 and also appeared in several episodes of NBC's *3rd Rock from the Sun* as Elman, a high school friend of the fictional alien-family's son. "Even though we didn't meet in an acting context, we shared a similar history," Lewis recalled of their near-instantaneous bond in London's *Independent* newspaper. "We felt failures as actors and we looked to each other for support."

Band forms in Los Angeles

Lewis and Sennett wrote two songs the first day they ever spent together in 1995, and they had a dozen songs finished at the end of that first week. In 1998 they decided to formally start a band. With Lewis as the vocalist and Sennett playing guitar, they recruited Pierre de Reeder, a bassist who Sennett knew from high school, and Dave Rock, a drummer. The band began playing small clubs in the Los Angeles area, and then released a self-titled debut and CD, titled *The Initial Friend,* on their own label in 1999. From there they went on the road, once spending an eight-month stretch driving around the United States in a van and playing shows. Two Rilo Kiley songs were featured in a small independent film released in 1999, called *Desert Blue,* which starred Christina Ricci (1980–) and Kate Hudson (1979–). In 2000, Lewis and Sennett appeared as themselves and with the band performing in an episode of the television show *Once and Again*. The show's creators were early fans of the band and invited them on to appear in a nightclub scene that had been written into the script of the ABC drama.

In 2001 Rilo Kiley released *Take Offs and Landings,* on the Seattle, Washington-based Barsuk Records label. But two other milestones happened that year, with potentially band-ending consequences: Dave Rock left the band, and Lewis and Sennett ended their romantic relationship. They found a replacement drummer, Jason Boesel, but also decided to take a few months off as a band. When they went back into the studio, there was still some tension between members. Once, there was an argument and Lewis stormed out, but then, as Sennett recalled, he felt something hit him in the back. It was a CD. "She had come back in just to throw something at me!" he recounted to Fiona Sturges in an interview with the London *Independent*. "So, yeah,

Former child star Blake Sennett found his calling as guitarist for Rilo Kiley. Tim Mosenfelder/Getty Images.

there were fights. But ultimately I love her more than anyone else in the world, so it doesn't matter. I think in the end we realised that it was music that brought us together, and it wasn't something that we wanted to abandon."

Rilo Kiley's next album, *The Execution of All Things,* marked their debut on an up-and-coming Nebraska label called

Saddle Creek. Omaha had recently earned some buzz as the next big alternative-music-scene city, and the Saddle Creek label was also the home of a budding singer-songwriter Conor Oberst (1980–), an Omaha native who would go on to indie-rock fame with his band Bright Eyes in 2004. Boesel was an occasional member of Oberst's band, and Oberst and Lewis became friends as well. The 2002 Rilo Kiley release earned a brief but career-making review in the *New York Times* in September 2002, with critic Kelefa Sanneh comparing it to their previous record, *Take Offs and Landings,* and finding it "just as sweet, but it's more self-assured, more adventurous and much more appealing." Sanneh also remarked that the band seemed to have evolved musically, and "the biggest change is in Ms. Lewis," Sanneh wrote, "who has learned to wield her sugary voice as a weapon."

Band members pursue other projects

Oftentimes Lewis's voice has earned comparisons to that of country-and-western legend Loretta Lynn (1935–), and Lewis admits she is a fan of country music and has been since a childhood spent listening to her mother's records. "What I'm drawn to is the simplicity of the songs but the complex nature of the lyrics," she explained to Jelbert in the *Times* of London article. "There are so many great stories." She still wrote songs on her own, but took some time off from Rilo Kiley to work with Ben Gibbard, of Death Cab for Cutie, members of which were Rilo Kiley's former labelmates at Barsuk Records. That side project, called the Postal Service, released *Give Up* in early 2003, and the band toured the United States and Europe.

Sennett also had taken some time off to pursue new musical directions. His band was called the Elected, and they released *Me First* in February 2004. Sennett had written the album's songs, while Lewis's work with the Postal Service had been limited to vocals, and she later admitted that Sennett's announcement that he was making a solo project worried her. "I was really afraid that Blake would leave and find that he could do exactly what he wanted elsewhere," she confessed to reporter Ben Wener. "But it turned out to be exactly the opposite. He took that experience and brought the best parts of it back to the band."

Rilo Kiley's third record, *More Adventurous*, caused somewhat of a stir in the close-knit indie-rock community, for it marked the band's major-label debut on Warner. They made the decision to leave Saddle Creek, they said, in order to reach a wider audience of potential fans, "have better distribution, and function as a band that wanted to do this for a little while," they jointly told Sturges. The record was still recorded in Nebraska, during a particularly cold spell in the winter of 2003–04, and came out in August 2004. The title was taken from a lyric of Lewis's, "I read that with every broken heart we should become more adventurous." Its first single and an MTV video, "Portions for Foxes," had a title borrowed from a biblical reference that had once caught Lewis's interest, an assertion that in the end, humans become food for animals when they die, though their souls move on. She admitted that much of her inspiration came from literary sources. "I started out enjoying just singing but now the sound is less important to me," she told Sandall in the *Daily Telegraph*. "It's just a means to get the words out."

Critics love *More Adventurous*

More Adventurous earned the band terrific reviews and was listed as one of the top ten releases of 2004 in several year-end critics' polls. "It's an intelligent and assured record, full of bitterly insightful lyrics that are as captivating as anything you'll hear this year," wrote Sturges. Her U.K. colleague in the *Daily Telegraph* asserted that "from the exuberantly ringing power pop of 'Portions for Foxes' to the country torch song 'I Never,' this collection marks Rilo Kiley's coming of age as songwriters, arrangers and performers." The *Philadelphia Inquirer* described Lewis as "a terrific conversational vocalist with a pert, agile soprano."

In the spring of 2005, Rilo Kiley played several well-attended shows, including the famed Coachella Festival in Indio, California, and the massive open-air Glastonbury

From Child Stars to Rock Stars

Both Jenny Lewis and Blake Sennett were working actors in Hollywood during their childhood and teen years. Lewis made her television debut in a 1985 episode of *The Twilight Zone,* and Sennett's came as Blake Soper in a *Highway to Heaven* episode during its 1986–87 season. Lewis went on to play troubled teens in several made-for-TV movies and won a supporting role in the 1998 Tobey Maguire-Reese Witherspoon feature film *Pleasantville.*

Sennett's most visible roles came in the Disney series *Boy Meets World* as Joey "The Rat" Epstein and in the hit NBC series *3rd Rock from the Sun.* "I wasn't very good at acting but I looked young for my age," he said years later in an interview with Fiona Sturges of London's *Independent* newspaper. "A 14-year-old [child actor] can legally work twice the hours of a 10-year-old, so looking young improves your prospects. But I never enjoyed it." Lewis also voiced mixed feelings about her early work when *Philadelphia Inquirer* writer Dan DeLuca quizzed her about it. "I feel grateful for the experience," she reflected, "but I wouldn't subject my children to it."

Festival in England. Even larger crowds turned out for the shows they played as the opening act for British chart-toppers Coldplay in late summer of 2005. Lewis's own solo project, tentatively titled *Rabbit Fur Coat* was slated for a 2006 release on Oberst's label, Team Love. On it, she worked with two Kentucky sisters, the Watson Twins, and assembled a tribute of sorts to a record from her mother's collection of vinyl that Lewis loved to play as a child. Titled *Gonna Take a Miracle,* the work was an unusual collaboration between a well-known but forgotten 1960s songwriter, Laura Nyro (1947–1997) and Labelle, the funky-soul act once fronted by television star Patti Labelle (1944–).

With their confessional lyrics and admissions to interviewers about the interpersonal difficulties they have experienced as a band over the years, there is little mystery about Rilo Kiley—except, it once seemed, for the origins of their name. They once said that it was in homage to two high school lovers, Ben Rilo and Stephen Kiley, who were football teammates but fulfilled a double suicide pact in 1909, but there is scant evidence of this story outside of articles and Web sites devoted to the band. Another rumor is that the name came from a dream that Sennett once had about an Irish person who foretold the day of

Lewis's death. "Different people make up different things, but it's actually a name from an old sports almanac, from our bass player's parent's house," Sennett finally said in an interview with Sarah Shanok for the *New York Press*. "It's not a very good story, so we have to make up other stories. You can blow the whistle."

For More Information

Periodicals

DeLuca, Dan. "Rilo Kiley's Lead Singer Leads with Her Heart." *Philadelphia Inquirer* (May 27, 2005).

Jelbert, Steve. "If at First You Succeed...." *Times* (London, England) (January 21, 2005): p. 15.

Messing, Nicholas. "Classic Rock, Teen Pop Grown Up and One Surprisingly Slowly Brewed Comeback." *Interview* (November 2002): p. 72.

Sandall, Robert. "Dark and Interesting Corners." *Daily Telegraph* (London, England) (January 22, 2005): p. 8.

Sanneh, Kelefa. "An Appealing Mix of Bitter and Sweet." *New York Times* (September 29, 2002): p. 29.

Shanok, Sarah. "Highlights: Listings." *New York Press* (October 5, 2004).

Sturges, Fiona. "Rock & Pop: Just Good Friends." *Independent* (London, England) (March 11, 2005): p. 14.

Wener, Ben. "Three Albums on, California Band Rilo Kiley Finally Is Breaking Big." *Orange County Register* (June 24, 2005).

Web Sites

Rilo Kiley Web Site. http://www.rilokiley.net/history/ (accessed on August 23, 2005).

Meg Rosoff

Bruno Vincent/Getty Images.

1958 • ***Boston, Massachusetts***

Writer

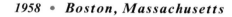

Meg Rosoff made a remarkable debut as a fiction writer with her 2004 novel for young adults, *How I Live Now*. It won several awards, and reviewers recommended it as a suitable book for adult readers, too. The story takes place in a war-ravaged England of the present day or near future and follows the adventures of Daisy, an American teenager who has come to stay with her British cousins. War breaks out not long after she arrives, and an unnamed foreign army occupies England. Later, the cousins must separate, and Daisy struggles to keep both her and her young cousin alive on a dangerous trek back to the family farm. "Rarely does a writer come up with a first novel so assured, so powerful and engaging that you can be pretty sure that you will want to read everything that this author is capable of writing," remarked critic Geraldine Bedell. "But that is what has happened with Meg Rosoff's *How I Live Now,* which, even before publication, is being talked of as a likely future classic."

Uneasy in suburbia

Rosoff was born in the late 1950s in Boston, Massachusetts. Her family was of Ashkenazi heritage, the segment of the Jewish diaspora (the mass dispersion of the Jews from their ancestral homeland of ancient Israel) who settled in eastern and central Europe. Her father, a surgeon, taught medicine at Harvard University, while Rosoff's mother was a psychiatric social worker. They lived in the Boston suburb of Newton, where Rosoff became a bookworm at an early age. "I knew my calling was writing at six or seven," she recalled in an interview with Meg

"Teens may feel that they have experienced a war themselves as they vicariously witness Daisy's worst nightmares .... Readers will emerge from the rubble much shaken."

Publishers Weekly **review of** *How I Live Now*

McCaffrey in *School Library Journal.* "Throughout my life, everyone would say, 'You should write a novel.' But, you know, I was never good at plot."

Rosoff was a self-described outcast in her teens, with curly hair when the fashion was for long and straight, and unathletic in a suburban setting where playing sports like tennis was a social obligation. "I was quite an uncomfortable teenager, very unattractive and looking for love," she recalled in an interview with Benedicte Page for *Bookseller.* In high school, she applied to Princeton University for college, but was turned down for admission, and so she entered Harvard University instead, where she majored in English and fine arts. Even there, she told Page, she felt like an outsider. "I hated that smug, 'We are Harvard and we are the best' attitude," she said in the *Bookseller* interview.

Rosoff was happier when she took some time off from her Harvard studies to live in England and take classes at Central St. Martin's College of Art and Design, a prestigious art school in London. She eventually returned to the United States, finished her degree, and settled in New York City, "and succumbed [gave in] to the fate of all bookish, over-educated girls: the Publishing Job," she joked in an article she wrote for London's *Guardian* newspaper. The piece chronicled her unhappy career experiences before she decided to write a novel: she was fired from her second job, spent two years at *People* magazine, and moved on to the *New York Times* with her former *People* boss. After that, she left journalism and publishing for the advertising world and spent fifteen years as a copywriter, both in New York City and then in London, to which she returned permanently in the late 1980s. But she rarely stayed at one company for very long. "I kept losing my job, mostly for being mouthy," she confessed to *Guardian* writer Julia Eccleshare. "I sounded off about everything."

Tragedy prompts career change

By 2001, Rosoff had married a painter—whom she had met during her first week in England in 1989—had a daughter, and was living in North London. She still worked, but asked for some time off from her job after her younger sister, Debby, died of breast cancer. She had an idea to write fiction, though she was unsure of how to do it. "I didn't know anything about writing a novel although I've been a fanatical reader all my life," she told *Sunday Times* journalist Amanda Craig. "I was used to writing what I thought were brilliant ads and then having a test-panel of housewives say they didn't like them."

As a kid, Rosoff had loved novels and stories about teenage girls and their beloved horses, and so she wrote a similar tale in the summer of 2002 and sent it to a literary-agent friend of her husband's. The agent passed on the story but asked to meet with Rosoff and suggested that she think about a different topic for her fiction. In the taxi on the way to that meeting, Rosoff came up with the idea for what became *How I Live Now*. "I was so grateful and so terrified, I wanted to impress her so much," Rosoff said to *Bookseller*. "And right on the way into lunch, I had this idea for a mad, eccentric family and their cousin who comes to live with them." The agent encouraged her to go ahead and start the project, but as Rosoff recalled in another interview, she was still unsure about how to do this. "What are the rules for writing a young adult novel?" she recalled asking the agent. "She told me there were no rules."

Three months later, Rosoff had completed the first draft of *How I Live Now*. Some of the wartime details were borrowed indirectly from the tales she heard from older Britons about their experiences during World War II (1939–45; war in which Great Britain, France, the United States, and their allies defeated Germany, Italy, and Japan). Other ideas were taken from present-day events, as British citizens grew nervous as United Kingdom forces readied to join a U.S.-led invasion of Iraq in early 2003 (U.S. president George W. Bush [1946–] and members of his administration believed that Saddam Hussein's regime harbored weapons of mass destruction, and may have even aided al-Qaeda at some point before that group's terrorist attacks in New York City and Washington, D.C., on September 11, 2001. The United Nations asked to see proof of this before permitting an invasion, but many leaders of other European nations were suspicious of the evidence presented.) The work was published by Penguin/Puffin Books in England in mid-2004, and in August of the same year in the United States by an imprint of Random House.

Novel set in wartime chaos

Rosoff's unlikely heroine is Daisy, a jaded New York City teen who has been treated for an eating disorder. Her mother died while giving birth to her, and her father has remarried. Daisy's stepmother, whom she calls Davina the Diabolical, is pregnant, and as the due-date nears, Daisy's father suggests a visit to meet her cousins from her mother's side in England—a plan clearly designed to get her out of the way. As the novel begins Daisy arrives to stay with her Aunt Penn, her mother's sister, and her four cousins. They live on a large rural property with goats and dogs and are a self-sufficient bunch unofficially headed by Obsert, the eldest boy. Next are twins, Edmond and Isaac, and a bossy nine-year-old girl named Piper. Daisy quickly notices that they all seem to be able to read one another's minds. Aunt Penn leaves them alone when she travels to Norway to participate in a peace conference organized with the hope of preventing an international political crisis, but one day bombs rock London. Aunt Penn is stranded in the Scandinavian country as England is occupied by an unnamed enemy army.

Daisy and Edmond, meanwhile, have fallen in love and are conducting a passionate love affair on the sly. The British Army seizes Aunt Penn's house, and Daisy and Piper are sent off to live with a farm family some distance away, while another place is found for the three boys. In time, a civilian uprising breaks out, and the occupying army reacts swiftly and begins to terrorize the countryside in its door-to-door search for insurgents. The girls are helped by kindly British soldiers and allowed to stay in army barracks, but when the enemy moves closer, Daisy and Piper flee into the woods. Daisy knows that Edmond and his brothers are at a place called Gateshead Farm, and she and Piper set out to make their way there on foot.

Thanks to Piper's knowledge of edible plants, the girls are able to stretch their army food-supply kit provisions until they come upon the river they know will take them to the Gateshead Farm. They find a horrific scene there, with dozens of corpses littering the landscape, and decide to return to Aunt Penn's house. There, they survive on the last remnants of the crops, and Daisy realizes that she has conquered the eating disorder—more an expression of her stubborn personality and unhappy home life, she freely admits—that had sent her into psychiatric care in her prior, pre-war life in New York. "One funny thing was that I didn't look much different now from the day I arrived in England," Daisy reflects, "but the difference was that now I ate what I could. Somewhere along the line I'd lost the will not to eat.... The idea of wanting to be thin in a world full of people dying from lack of good struck even me as stupid."

Story reveals home hardships

Though many of the political details of the war are unclear, there is a slow unfolding of events that serves to show how it came to affect the lives of Daisy and her cousins. Having to leave pets behind when their home is taken over by the British Army is just one detail. "I wanted readers to know what it was like to live through a war because I wanted them to get past the 'over there' syndrome," Rosoff explained to Ilene Cooper in a *Booklist* article. "There's such a tendency to look at people who aren't like you and think they don't suffer the way you do. The best letter I received was from a girl who said, 'Your book made me realize what it was like to live in a country where there's war.' That's exactly what I set out to do."

How I Live Now won two notable honors: the *Guardian* Children's Fiction Prize in the United Kingdom, and the Michael L. Printz Award for excellence in literature for young adults from the American Library Association. Rosoff's debut became one of the most highly recommended books of 2004 on both sides of the Atlantic, and the film rights were sold almost immediately upon publication. Though written as a young adult novel, many reviewers asserted that it possessed great "crossover" appeal for adult readers, too. Mark Haddon, one of the judges of the *Guardian* newspaper's annual book awards and himself the author of a crossover novel, *The Curious Incident of the Dog in the Night-Time*, hailed it as "that rare, rare thing, a first novel with a sustained, magical and utterly faultless voice," according to the London *Evening Standard*.

Rosoff had also written a children's picture book before setting out to write her first novel. Inspired in part by her young daughter, Rosoff penned a tale about a quartet of misbehaving boars, or wild pigs—Boris, Morris, Horace, and Doris—and the little boy and girl who try to point them in a more sociable direction. When the contract to publish *Meet Wild Boars* was finalized after an auction among British and American publishers, Rosoff quit her advertising job. The title was published in early 2005 in the United States, with illustrations from Sophie Blackall, whom Rosoff knew from her advertising days.

Tragedy strikes again

Yet as *How I Live Now* was winning rave reviews and literary honors, Rosoff was in the hospital undergoing treatment for breast cancer. She had been so busy in the pre-publication whirl that she missed her annual mammogram, the screening test for this form of cancer. "Then they found it," she told the *Sunday Times*. "Two of my sisters have had a particularly aggressive form of the cancer. You don't get a prognosis about whether you're going to live. I'm halfway through my chemotherapy and with each dose it gets worse. It doesn't hurt but you feel nauseated the week after so that even cranberry juice makes you feel sick because it's the same colour as the medication." Still, Rosoff's realistic outlook and somewhat cynical nature helped her put her situation into perspective. "I'm not a worrier. When people rang up and said, 'What a tragedy, your family is so unlucky,' I said that I expected it," she said. "You don't get through life without something terrifying happening."

Rosoff plans to continue her second, far more satisfying career as an author. In the article she wrote for the *Guardian* about her years in advertising, she wrote that "the first question everyone asks is: Don't you wish you'd done it sooner? And the obvious answer is: no. If I'd written my first novel 20 years ago, I'd still be trying to get it published today. It would have emerged tortured, humourless, and overlong; a thinly disguised autobiography attracting enough rejection to cause permanent psychological damage.... Above all, I wouldn't have had the pleasure of not working in advertising—possibly the best thing about writing books. "

For More Information

Books

Rosoff, Meg. *How I Live Now*. New York: Wendy Lamb Books/ Random House, 2004.

Periodicals

Bedell, Geraldine. "Review: Books: Fiction: Suddenly Last Summer." *Observer* (London, England) (July 25, 2004): p. 16.

Cooper, Ilene. "Meg Rosoff." *Booklist* (March 15, 2005): p. 1289.

Craig, Amanda. "Suffering? It's How I Live Now." *Sunday Times* (London, England) (November 14, 2004): p. 5.

Davey, Douglas P. Review of *How I Live Now. School Library Journal* (September 2004): p. 216.

Eccleshare, Julia. "Saturday Review: Childrens Fiction." *Guardian* (London, England) (October 9, 2004): p. 33.

"Living It Up." *Bookseller* (November 19, 2004): p. 15.

Mattson, Jennifer. "Review of *How I Live Now*." *Booklist* (September 1, 2004): p. 123.

McCaffrey, Meg. "Answering the Call." *School Library Journal* (March 2005): p. 46.

Page, Benedicte. "Living Through Wartime." *Bookseller* (June 4, 2004): p. 28.

Review of *How I Live Now. Publishers Weekly* (July 5, 2004): p. 56.

Review of *Meet Wild Boars. Publishers Weekly* (March 28, 2005): p. 78.

Rosoff, Meg. "Saturday Review: Commentary: How I Jumped out of the Sack Race." *Guardian* (London, England) (November 20, 2004): p. 7.

Sexton, David. "Dabbling in Disaster." *Evening Standard* (London, England) (August 2, 2004): p. 65.

Web Sites

Bookbrowse: Author Biography. http://www.bookbrowse.com/biographies/index.cfm?author_number = 1059 (accessed on August 23, 2005).

Angela Ruggiero

January 3, 1980 • *Panorama City, California*

Hockey player

Angela Ruggiero made hockey history in 2005 when she skated onto the ice wearing a Tulsa Oilers jersey during a home game of the Central Hockey League team. That January night, she became the first woman ever to play a non-goalie position during a men's professional hockey match in North America. Ruggiero is a two-time Olympic skilled defense player, and she is considered one of the most impressive new women athletes in the sport. As her college career on Harvard University's women's team came to a close in 2004, she was honored with the Patty Kazmaier Award, given to the top women's college hockey player in the United States.

Joins brother in youth league

Ruggiero was not the only member of her family to make hockey history at Tulsa's Maxwell Convention Center during that 2005 game: Her brother, Bill Ruggiero (1981–), is the Oilers' goalie, and together they became the first brother-sister combination ever to play on the same team in professional hockey. Bill is thirteen months younger than Angela, who was born on January 3, 1980, and was the reason his father, also named Bill, went to the Pasadena Ice Chalet one day in 1987 to sign him up for a youth hockey league. The family lived in Simi Valley, a part of Ventura County that borders the large San Fernando Valley of greater Los Angeles. Bill Sr. was originally from Connecticut, where he had played hockey during his own childhood. He was surprised to learn how expensive the game had become, even at the youth level, but was told that the Pasadena league offered a

> **"**If the young girls saw the hitting right away, I think they would be frightened and not get involved. Right now, the women's game is developing an identity of its own.**"**

family discount—the more siblings who enrolled, the cheaper the fee per child. Bill Sr. decided to sign up his son as well as Angela and her sister Pam that day.

Angela Ruggiero didn't yet know how to skate, but she proved a quick learner. "When I first stepped out on the ice, I started to cry," she recalled in an interview with the *Daily News*. "Then somebody told me to hold onto the boards and push my feet forward, and by the time I left (practice) I knew how to skate." She emerged as a strong player and even a fearless one rather quickly. "She was pretty tough," a former coach, Scott Plummer, told the *Daily News*. "She was the only girl I coached, and she was one of our top players."

At the age of thirteen, Ruggiero began playing on an all-girls' team in suburban Los Angeles. Her skills on the ice remained above average, and she became known as "the Terminator." When she was fourteen, her parents moved to

Milestones in Women's Hockey

1890: The daughter of Lord Stanley (1841–1908), the Governor General of Canada, is photographed playing hockey with her brothers on the rink at Rideau Hall, the official Ottawa residence of the Governor General. Lord Stanley is an important promoter of the sport in Canada, and later the championship cup of the National Hockey League will be named in his honor.

1892: Barrie, Ontario is the site of the first organized all-women's hockey game.

1894: A women's team formed at Queen's University in Kingston, Ontario, is criticized by some school authorities as inappropriate. The women play in turtleneck sweaters and ankle-length wool skirts over their skates.

1920s–1930s: Women's hockey becomes popular in Canada, and a league takes shape. A southwestern Ontario powerhouse, the Preston Rivulettes dominate the ice in the 1930s. Between 1930 and 1939, when a coming world war brought an end to the league, the Rivulettes enjoy an astonishing run, losing just two games out of 350 played.

1956: An Ontario Supreme Court decision bars a nine-year-old girl, Abby Hoffman, from a youth league. Hoffman had cut her hair short and pretended to be a boy in order to play. When she was caught and cut from the team, her parents challenged the league's "boys only" rule, but the league's policy was upheld by the provincial high court.

1967: The first Dominion Ladies Hockey Tournament is held in Brampton, Ontario.

1970s: Female hockey programs gain popularity across Canada and at U.S. colleges and universities.

1982: The first national championship for women's ice hockey is held in Canada.

1990: The International Ice Hockey Federation (IIHF) establishes the Women's World Championship series. The Canadian team wins nearly every year.

1990–91: USA Hockey, the governing body for amateur ice hockey in the United States, counts 2,700 female players in the sport.

1992: Olympic officials announce that women's hockey will become a medal sport at the 1998 Winter Games scheduled to be held in Nagano, Japan.

1993–94: USA Hockey counts 6,300 female players.

1997–98: USA Hockey reports 23,010 female players were counted for the season.

1998: Women's hockey becomes an Olympic medal sport at the Winter Games in Nagano, Japan, with the U.S. women winning a stunning victory over the Canadian national team.

1999: Canada's National Women's Hockey League (NWHL) is founded.

2003: Hayley Wickenheiser (1978–), a former Canadian national women's team player and three-time Olympian, joins the Kirkkonummi Salamat, a men's professional team in Finland. She becomes the first woman to score a point in a male professional hockey league.

2005: Number of U.S. female hockey players reaches 52,469.

Michigan, but she wanted to play high school hockey at a school with a strong women's program and chose a prestigious private school, Choate Rosemary Hall in Wallingford, Connecticut. She spent the next four years there, seeing her parents only on school holidays or when they came to visit her in Connecticut. Though the school did not offer athletic scholarships, it did provide financial aid for students to help with the tuition costs that reached $35,360 in the 2004–05 academic year. Its alumni include U.S. president John F. Kennedy (1917–1963; served 1961–63), and Ruggiero attended the school around the same time as Ivanka Trump (1981–), daughter of Manhattan real-estate mogul Donald Trump (1946–) and Amanda Hearst, an heiress of the Hearst newspaper fortune.

Wins Olympic gold

By the time she reached Choate, Ruggiero was so skilled a player that she easily won a place on the girls' varsity team, and she was its only freshman member. The team went on to win a league championship with her help, and she also perfected her game by playing on a club team, Connecticut Polar Bears Pee-Wees, one of the top girls' teams in the country in the thirteen-to-fifteen (Pee Wee) division. The Polar Bears won the U.S. National Women's Championship in 1995, and that same year Ruggiero earned a spot on the U.S. national junior team. At the age of fifteen, she became the youngest player on the 1996 U.S. women's national hockey team. "It's a great feeling to make a team like that even though I'm still so young," Ruggiero told Vincent Bonsignore of the *Daily News*. "I earned my spot on the team and I earned their respect."

During her years at Choate, Ruggiero earned excellent grades and served as class president for three of her four years there. On the ice, she set several school records, including the most goals (40), assists (23), and points (63). Olympic-level hockey was the next step, and she won a spot on the U.S. women's Olympic ice hockey team for the 1998 Winter Games at Nagano, Japan. Her teammates included several young women she had known from the previous national team, including Cammi Granato (1971–), another leading American player.

The Nagano Games marked the first time that women's ice hockey became a full-medal Olympic sport, which was a significant milestone for the game and its growing numbers of female players. The U.S. team beat Canada for the gold medal that year, a stunning victory against a Canadian women's powerhouse team that they had lost to in every major tournament before that.

As one of the top American players of her gender, Ruggiero was courted by the women's hockey programs of several prominent universities, and she chose Harvard over Brown, Dartmouth, and the University of Minnesota. She majored in anthropology at Harvard, but took a year-long break to train for the 2002 Olympics, which were held in Salt Lake City, Utah. She was selected as one of the eight athletes who would carry the American flag during the opening ceremonies. This flag, however, was special: it was a tattered one that had been found in the rubble of the World Trade Center after September 11, 2001 (the devastating attacks on the New York City skyscraper towers as well as the Pentagon in Washington, D.C., that were carried out by members of al-Qaeda). The flag-bearers were chosen because of some personal connection to the tragedy. In Ruggiero's case, her friend and U.S. national teammate Kathleen Kauth (1979–) had lost her father in the World Trade Center attack. Three months after the disaster, Kauth was cut from the U.S. women's Olympic team when it had to be reduced to twenty members. Ruggiero was honored to take Kauth's place as a flag-bearer in the opening ceremonies, which she described to Matt McHale as "a powerful moment, so emotional. One of the policemen nearby told me to be strong. Then the Mormon Tabernacle Choir sang the national anthem like I've never heard it."

Earns Harvard degree

Ruggiero and her Olympic teammates won the silver medal at the 2002 Salt Lake City Games, losing the gold to the strong Canadian women's team. They had been favored to win the gold again, however, because the U.S. team, on a year-long international tour, had compiled a 32–0 record and beat the Canadians a total of eight times over the last few months. Now in her early twenties and no longer the youngest player on the

Angela Ruggiero handles the puck during a game in the 2005 Women's World Ice Hockey Championships. Jeff Gross/ Getty Images.

team, Ruggiero earned high marks from sportswriters for her athleticism and grace on the ice. McHale called her development "a successful blend of speed with a physical style rarely seen in the women's game. In the NHL, they call it playing with an edge."

Ruggiero returned to her studies at Harvard in 2002. The 2003–04 season was her final one and her team made it to post-season play, the National Collegiate Athletic Association women's hockey semifinals and finals that are known as the "Frozen Four." Harvard lost the championship to the University of Minnesota, 6–2, but once again Ruggiero ended her school career as a record-holder at Harvard. She racked up honors for the most goals scored by a defensive player in a single game (5), most goals by a defensive player in a season (29), most goals by a defensive player in a career (79), and another record for most points by a defensive player in a career (214). That last one is thought to be a collegiate best for players of either gender.

Ruggiero also finished her collegiate career as the winner of the 2004 Patty Kazmaier Award, given to the best women's collegiate hockey player in the country. The award is named in honor of a top 1980s Princeton University player who died in 1990. After graduation, Ruggiero spent some time with her family in suburban Detroit, but she joined the Tulsa Oilers for one game in January 2005 thanks to her brother, Bill. He had turned professional in 2002 and was the goalie for the Oilers, a team in the Central Hockey League. This is a "minors" professional league, in comparison to the major-league National Hockey League (NHL). The team found itself short a player on the defensive line, and Bill jokingly suggested to his teammates that his sister should fill in. Team executives liked the idea, and Ruggiero was signed to a one-game contract. She skated onto the ice on January 28, 2005, in a match against the Rio Grande Valley Killer Bees. She had one assist, the statistical record for one or two players who pass the puck to a teammate, who scores a goal with it in next shot.

Rejoins brother on the ice

Ruggiero entered the record books for women's hockey as the first woman to play in a professional game outside of the goalie crease. In 1992, Manon Rhéaume (1972–) played one pre-season game as goalie for the Tampa Bay Lightning; four years later Erin Whitten took an eighteen-second ceremonial skate with a team in the minor United Hockey League (UHL), the Flint Generals of Michigan. But Ruggiero was the first to play a regular-season game as a full team member, though it was just a one-time event. She and Bill were also the first brother-sister combination in professional hockey, and they even appeared in a segment on NBC's highly rated morning news broadcast, *The Today Show*. Ruggiero told correspondent Kevin Tibbles that she would be skating for all women players that day. "They're here to see if I can keep up with the boys," she joked, but she also called it the "chance of a lifetime. I'm just going to go out there the last shift and get a point. And then be able to go down and tap my brother on the pads and give him a hug, you know. I'll remember that for the rest of my life."

Later that year, in April 2005, Ruggiero scored the winning goal that determined the champion of the Women's World Ice Hockey Championships in an overtime shootout, when each team sends five players to take their turn trying to score against the opposing team's goalie. Once again, Ruggiero's U.S. team had reached the finals with their Canadian archrivals, and this time won their first-ever victory in the Women's World Ice Hockey Championships since this International Ice Hockey Federation (IIHF) women's tournament began in 1990. Ruggiero had also spent the year wearing her number 4 jersey with the East Coast Wizards, an elite Boston-area women's team that often played against top Junior men's teams.

Though a women's professional hockey league was a hoped-for goal for Ruggiero and her former Olympic and national teammates, she was thrilled that hockey had brought her so many riches already. She had received a terrific education and traveled around the world to play the game she loved. "I've had all this opportunity," she reflected in a *Sports Illustrated for Women* interview. "Our family didn't have much money, but my dad's and mom's paychecks went to hockey. I was brought up to appreciate things. Most of my friends at Harvard have tons of money and travel all the time. My sister's never been out of the country, unless you count Canada."

For More Information

Periodicals

Bonsignore, Vincent. "Ice-Hockey Prodigy Skating Her Way to Fame." *Daily News* (Los Angeles) (April 10, 1996): p. T4.

Connolly, John. "Harvard's Ruggiero Top of the Line." *Boston Herald* (December 8, 2003): p. 80.

"Facing Up: She's a Girl Not a Goon." *Tampa Tribune* (February 8, 1998): p. 1.

Farber, Michael. "Her Body of Work." *Sports Illustrated for Women* (January 1, 2001): p. 94.

Fees, Jarre. "Breaking the Ice." *Daily News* (Los Angeles) (January 17, 1998): p. S1.

International Wire. "The *Today Show* transcript for Tuesday, February 1, 2005."

McHale, Matt. "Simi Product Plays Hockey 'With an Edge.'" *Daily News* (Los Angeles) (February 12, 2002): p. S1.

Pote, Jamie. "March Madness; Harvard Notebook; Ruggiero Ends Career at Top of Her Game." *Boston Herald* (March 29, 2004): p. 86.

Web Sites

Angela Ruggiero. http://gocrimson.collegesports.com/sports/w-hockey/mtt/ruggiero_angela00.html (accessed on August 23, 2005).

Girls'/Women's Hockey. http://www.usahockey.com/girlswomen/main_site/main/home/ (accessed on August 23, 2005).

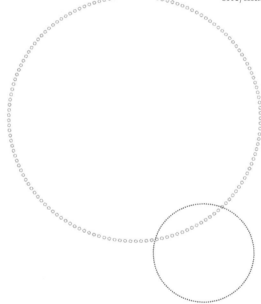

Maria Sharapova

April 19, 1987 • *Nyagan, Siberia, Soviet Union*

Tennis player

In the summer of 2004, seventeen-year-old Maria Sharapova became the first Russian player to win Wimbledon, the prestigious tennis event that takes place every summer in London, England. Wimbledon is one of the four Grand Slam events in tennis, along with the U.S., French, and Australian Open tournaments, and winners of these contests have triumphed over the best players in the world. Sharapova, who had spent much of her life in Florida at a renowned tennis academy, was the third youngest champion in Wimbledon history, and her women's singles Wimbledon title came with a $1 million prize purse. Afterward, she was signed to a number of product endorsement deals. By the summer of 2005, she had won a spot on *Forbes* magazine's Celebrity 100 list as the highest paid female athlete in the world.

Says good-bye to mother

Born on April 19, 1987, Sharapova is the daughter of Yuri and Yelena Sharapova. Her father worked in the construction industry, and both parents were avid athletes. They had met in Gomel, a city in the Ukraine that was near the Chernobyl nuclear reactor, the site of the world's worst nuclear accident in April 1986, just a year before Sharapova was born. When her mother became pregnant, she and Yuri decided to move east to escape the potentially damaging radioactive effects of the accident. They settled in Nyagan, Siberia, where Sharapova was born. Yuri

> **"Tennis obviously is going to make my money at this point, and that's what I've been practicing for. But it's not my life."**

found work in the Siberian oilfields, but the climate was too cold for them. They saved their money for four years and finally were able to move to Sochi, a pleasant resort town on the Black Sea in the south of Russia.

Sharapova's parents liked to play tennis, and they gave her a racket as a toddler and began teaching her how to hit the ball. Because they could not afford a genuine child-size racket, they cut off the handle of an adult one for her to master instead. She proved a quick learner, and when she was six years old they traveled to Moscow for a youth tennis clinic. One of the celebrity athletes at the event was Czech-born Martina Navratilova (1956–), a nine-time women's singles winner at Wimbledon. Navratilova was impressed by Sharapova's skills and suggested to the parents that they contact the Nick Bollettieri Tennis Academy in Bradenton, Florida. This was a tennis-focused boarding school that had trained several future champions, including Andre Agassi (1970–), Pete Sampras (1971–), and Monica Seles (1973–).

The Sharapovas decided to go to Florida and try to get Maria enrolled there. But only Yuri could get a visa (a document permitting a foreign citizen to legally enter the country) to travel to the United States, and so Yelena stayed behind in Sochi and waited for her visa application to be approved. They also needed money for the trip and had to borrow several hundred dollars from Yuri and Yelena's parents. This was an enormous sum for her parents, partly because Russia was in a state of financial chaos at the time, and average working families like hers struggled to obtain the basic necessities of life in the new, non-Communist era in which the state did not generously provide jobs, housing, and healthcare for all citizens. "My parents weren't stupid," Sharapova told Peter Kafka in *Forbes*. "The conditions in Russia weren't the best for tennis."

Wins scholarship

In 1994 Sharapova and her father arrived at the Bollettieri Tennis Academy in Bradenton, but they were told that admission to the school was by invitation only, and that the seven-year-old girl was too young to enter anyway. They remained in Florida, and a coach was found for her while her father worked as a waiter and took odd jobs to support them. She learned English in just four months, and her tennis skills steadily improved. At the age of nine, she and her father went back to the Bollettieri Academy, and she proved herself so well on a tryout that she was given a full scholarship to the $46,000-a-year school. The Academy was part of the International Management Group (IMG), a talent agency that handled the careers of entertainers and athletes, and its scouts likely recognized Sharapova's potential for future stardom.

Around this same time, Yelena Sharapova finally received her visa and was able to join her husband and daughter, ending a two-year separation. But when Sharapova entered the Bollettieri Academy, she had to live in its boarding school. She later hinted in interviews that it was a tough, competitive atmosphere, and she was sometimes the target of bullying by the older girls. Her days included regular academic classes and as many as six hours a day on the tennis courts in practice sessions. At the age of eleven, she signed on with coach Robert Lansdorp, who had

Perhaps the World's Poshest Sporting Event

Maria Sharapova's stunning victory over Serena Williams (1981–) at Wimbledon in 2004 made the Russian-born player the third youngest winner in the history of the tournament. Wimbledon, watched by millions of television viewers all over the world, is considered one of the world's most prestigious sporting events. Officially, the Grand Slam event is known as "The Championships, Wimbledon," and is held annually in the town of Wimbledon, a part of the Greater London metropolitan area.

The first Wimbledon tennis championship was held in the summer of 1877, and the All England Lawn Tennis and Croquet Club was its sponsor. The event included only men's singles, though they were known for many years as "gentlemen's" singles. Ladies' singles and gentlemen's doubles events were added in 1884.

The present rye-grass courts of Wimbledon, located off Church Road, have been host to the annual event since 1922. There are nineteen courts in all, with Centre Court hosting the finals matches. But the grass surface has proved an extremely difficult one for some of the world's top-ranked players, because the ball's bounce is not as high as on a clay court. Players who adopt the serve-and-volley technique—in which they make their serve, then rush toward the net to hit the next shot as a volley—tend to fare better on grass courts.

Wimbledon still has many quaint English traditions. All umpires, officials, and court associates wear uniforms of the official Wimbledon colors, green and purple. The dress code for players is a strict one, with tennis whites strongly suggested, and female players are still referred to as "Miss" or "Mrs." in official announcements. Until 2003, all Centre Court players had to bow or curtsy toward the Royal Box, where members of the Royal Family watch the game, when they came onto the court. Now they are expected to do so only if the Queen or the Prince of Wales is in the Royal Box that day. Rain delays, common to the English summer, often delay matches for hours or even days. Strawberries and cream are the unofficial snack food of the event.

Members of the British royal family are not the only famous faces in the Wimbledon crowd. Movie stars, heads of state, and celebrity athletes from other sports can also be spotted. The most photographed couple in 2005 were film stars Jude Law (1972–) and his fiancée, Sienna Miller (1981–).

guided the careers of Sampras as well as Tracy Austin (1962–), a two-time U.S. Open winner, and Lindsay Davenport (1976–), who won three Grand Slam events between 1998 and 2000. Sharapova also signed with IMG around this time, and this paved the way for her first deal with Nike, the athletic shoe and clothing maker.

Sharapova won her first junior championship title at the age of thirteen. Two years later, she made it to the finals of the Australian Open Junior championship, which was her best ranking in tennis to date, and entered her first adult professional tournament in Tokyo, Japan, in September 2003. In the finals of that event, she defeated Aniko Kapros (1983–) of Hungary. A month later, she won an event in Quebec City, Canada, and in June 2004 beat Tatiana Golovin (1988–), a fellow Russian player and former Bollettieri schoolmate, at a Birmingham, England tournament.

Makes tennis history

Two weeks later, Sharapova made her second appearance at Wimbledon. She had played it a year earlier, in 2003, but lost in an early round to Svetlana Kuznetsova (1985–), another emerging Russian player. When Sharapova began at Wimbledon in 2004, she was "seeded," or ranked by the Wimbledon executive committee, as thirteenth among women players in the world. This meant that there were twelve other players with more wins, and more experience on the court, but she steadily advanced through the quarterfinals and semifinals. She became the first Russian tennis player to reach a Wimbledon final since 1974, when a woman named Olga Morosova did so.

Of the four Grand Slam events, the Wimbledon tournament is the only one that is played on a grass court, not a clay one. It seemed to give Sharapova an advantage, noted *New York Times* writer Christopher Clarey. "Sharapova's big game is ideally suited to grass," Clarey asserted. "She hits relatively flat, favors slice serves over high-kicking topspin serves and clearly enjoys moving on a surface that leaves many players frustrated." In the women's singles finals, Sharapova beat two-time Wimbledon champion Serena Williams (1981–). At seventeen years and two months, Sharapova became the third youngest winner in the history of Wimbledon, which dated back to 1877. At the post-tournament press conference, she said that "it's always been my dream to come here and to win," the *New York Times* report quoted her as saying, "but it was never in my mind that I would do it this year."

Sharapova became an instant international celebrity. Sportswriters announced that she could be the next major women's star in tennis, and her win was notable for what some

Maria Sharapova stretches to return a forehand from Venus Williams in their women's singles semi-final match at the 2005 Wimbledon Championships.
© Kieran Doherty/Reuters/Corbis.

believed to be the end of an era for the Williams sisters, Serena, and her equally talented sister Venus (1980–): when Sharapova beat Serena at Wimbledon, it marked the first time since 1999 that neither Williams sister was holding a Grand Slam singles title. *Sports Illustrated* put Sharapova on its July 19 cover, and a week later featured a lengthy article on her rise to the top of her game. Writer L. Jon Wertheim called her "ebullient, bilingual and hyperconfident—not to mention tall, blonde and beautiful," and asserted she "had suddenly become, as Martina Navratilova put it, 'the best thing that could have happened' to women's tennis."

Eliminated at next Grand Slam event

The U.S. Open was the next Grand Slam event in the 2004 season. This contest is held in Flushing Meadows, New York, just outside

New York City. Anticipation among tennis lovers to see how Sharapova would do ran high as the event got underway. She did poorly, however, losing to Mary Pierce (1975–) in the third round. Later that year, Sharapova's game improved, and she beat Serena Williams at the season-ending Women's Tennis Association (WTA) Tour Championship.

Sharapova had spent some of the rain delays at Wimbledon studying for her high school diploma, which she earned with the help of an online curriculum program for home-schooled students. In April 2005 she celebrated her eighteenth birthday in New York City at a trendy nightclub called Hiro. The bash was paid for by cell-phone maker Motorola, with whom she had signed an endorsement deal just after her Wimbledon victory the year before. It was one of several generous contracts that Sharapova's IMG agent negotiated for her. These included a renewal of the Nike endorsement, a deal with camera-maker Canon, another with luxury-watch maker Tag Heuer, and one with personal-care products giant Colgate-Palmolive. There was even her own fragrance line in the works. The combined endorsement deals gave Sharapova an income of $18.2 million, according to *Forbes* magazine, which ranked her as fifty-seventh on its "Celebrity 100" list in June 2005.

Sharapova spent $2.7 million of those earnings on a 4,700-square-foot home for herself and her parents in Bradenton, Florida. She continued to train for more Grand Slam events over the winter. In early 2005, she lost in the semifinals of the Australian Open to Serena Williams, and at Stade Roland Garros, the red-clay court Paris stadium that hosts the French Open every May, she lost in the quarterfinals to Belgium's Justine Henin-Hardenne (1982–). At Wimbledon a month later, she failed to keep her title, losing in the semifinals to Venus Williams. "I don't think I played my best tennis," she told reporters at the post-game press conference. She also said that Williams had "hit a lot of hard, deep balls. She was serving consistently big."

"I'm not the new anyone"

Sharapova is often compared to Anna Kournikova (1981–), a slightly older Russian player, also an attractive blonde like

Sharapova, who was hailed as the next big star when she was just sixteen years old. Kournikova also won a number of well-paying endorsement contracts early in her career but, unlike Sharapova, failed to win any major titles in tennis. Known for her romances with hockey player Sergei Federov (1969–) and pop singer Enrique Iglesias (1975–), Kournikova played her last major tennis tournament in April 2003. Serious analysts of the sport, however, note there are few similarities between the two Russian players beyond their model-like, blonde looks. Sharapova has sometimes responded to the comparisons with a sharp remark in interviews. "I'm not the new anyone and certainly not the new Kournikova," she said in a *Times* article during Wimbledon 2004. "I'm the new Maria Sharapova. People seem to forget that Anna isn't in the picture any more. It's Maria time now. You cannot compare us anyway. After all, she never won a single tournament."

Sharapova hopes to take her second women's singles title at Wimbledon and perhaps even a "Grand Slam"—winning Wimbledon plus the Australian, French, and U.S. Opens in the same year. No other female player has done so since German champion Steffi Graf (1969–) in 1988. Sharapova also looks forward to a career beyond tennis. She has done some modeling, is a devoted reader of fashion magazines, and has even helped design some of her court outfits with Nike. Fashion design might even be a career option when she retires from tennis, which she told *Vogue* writer Dodie Kazanjian she planned to do in her mid-twenties. Acting would be another option. "Nothing scares me," she told Kazanjian, "because I'm not worried about failure. You never know until you try. So if you don't try, you've failed. All I know is, I'm starving to be the best."

For More Information

Periodicals

Burt, Jason. "Tennis: Wimbledon 2004: Girl Who Came in from the Cold after Friday Night Fever." *Independent Sunday* (London, England) (July 4, 2004): p. 2.

Clarey, Christopher. "Sharapova Conquers Wimbledon." *New York Times* (July 4, 2004): p. SP1.

Kafka, Peter. "The Hot Shot." *Forbes* (July 4, 2005): p. 116.

Kazanjian, Dodie. "The New Hit Girl." *Vogue* (March 2005): p. 544.

Price, S.L. "Youth Movement." *Sports Illustrated* (July 7, 2003): p. 72.

Roberts, John. "Tennis: Wimbledon 2005: Williams Rolls Back the Years to Dethrone Golden Sharapova." *Independent* (London, England) (July 1, 2005): p. 72.

Wertheim, L. Jon. "A Star (Who Happens to Be a Gorgeous 6-Foot Blonde with Blistering Strokes) Is Born." *Sports Illustrated* (July 26, 2004): p. 58.

Woolcock, Nicola, and Ashling O'Connor. "Living the Dream from Siberia to SW19." *Times* (London, England) (July 3, 2004): p. 3.

Web Sites

Maria Sharapova (RUS). http://www.wtatour.com/players/player-profiles/PlayerBio.asp?ID = &EntityID = 1&CustomerID = 0&OrderID = 0&ReturnURL = /&PlayerID = 310137 (accessed on August 23, 2005).

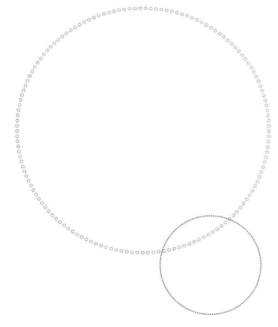

Jeff Skoll

January 16, 1965 • Montreal, Quebec, Canada

Philanthropist, chief executive officer

Jeff Skoll was the first employee of the online auction Web site eBay. As president during its crucial early years of the mid-1990s, Skoll was a key player in the growth of the company from one of the first financial phenomenons of the new Internet age to a literal online community, with millions of users around the world. But Skoll, a Canadian with a strong social conscience, bowed out of the business world at an early age and began to devote his time to philanthropy, or donating large sums of his personal wealth to worthy charitable causes. He still holds a stake in eBay, just less than 8 percent, and in 2005 those personal stock holdings were valued at $3.7 billion. With his wealth he has funded the Skoll Foundation, which has over $500 million in assets. The foundation gives grants to socially responsible business ventures and funds charitable projects around the world.

Father's illness a turning point

Skoll was born in January 1965 in the French-Canadian city of Montreal. He was in his teens when his family moved to Toronto, Ontario, where his father owned a company that supplied industrial chemicals to businesses. His dad came home one day with news that he had been diagnosed with cancer of the kidney. "I remember my dad saying that he wasn't so sad that he might die, but he was sad that he'd never done the things that he'd wanted to do in life," Skoll recalled in an interview with Thomas Watson for *Canadian Business*. His father survived the illness, but the event had a lasting impact on Skoll, who was a teenager at the time. He

> **"I never really expected to have a ton of money. As it happened, eBay kind of worked out."**

vowed that he would never face the same dilemma, the realization that he had put his career ahead of his personal goals.

Skoll wanted to become a writer. He thought, however, that he should first earn enough money to live comfortably, so that he could pursue that goal without the stress of needing to succeed financially in it. With the idea of making some money during his twenties and then retiring early, he studied electrical engineering at the University of Toronto. After he earned his degree in 1987, he founded a computer consulting firm, and he also had a lucrative computer rental business. Realizing that he was short on the management skills needed to run a successful business, he went back to school and earned a Master of Business Administration (M.B.A.) degree. He was accepted into the prestigious graduate business school of Stanford University in Palo Alto, California.

Moving to America was something of a culture shock for Skoll. Though there were street people in Canadian cities like Toronto, he was stunned to see the numbers of homeless in nearby San Francisco and even in smaller cities clustered south of the San Francisco Bay Area, where U.S. high-tech companies were flourishing. Individual Canadians, and Canadian businesses, paid higher taxes than their American counterparts, and those tax dollars funded a social service network designed to help the disadvantaged; they also helped to finance a universal health care system for all. Skoll became editor of the Stanford business school's student newspaper, *The Reporter,* and began to write about the gap between the rich and the poor in the world, and what a new generation of business-school graduates—his generation—might do to close it.

"A stupid idea"

Skoll earned his M.B.A. degree from Stanford in 1995. He took a job in nearby San Jose with Knight-Ridder Information, a division of the American newspaper chain, as manager of its distribution channels. That same year, a casual acquaintance of his, a computer programmer named Pierre Omidyar (1967–), launched an Internet site he called Auction Web. Omidyar had written a unique software program for it, and he thought that he might be able to use sales of that software to finance a larger online empire of Internet-user services. One day, he told Skoll about his plan. "First he told me it was a stupid idea," Omidyar recalled in an article he wrote about Skoll for *Time International,* "and then he agreed to come on board."

Omidyar initially hired Skoll to write a business plan, a lengthy formal document that fledgling entrepreneurs must show to bank loan officers or potential private investors. When eBay was officially born as a company late in 1995, Skoll was the first employee listed on the payroll. The eBay name came from Omidyar's first company, Echo Bay Consulting Services, and he and Skoll saw it as merely the name of the holding company for the planned empire. But eBay's auction site began to catch on quickly, gaining thousands of new users each month. Most were buyers and sellers of various collectibles, such as the popular Beanie Baby toys, but soon others began to sell vintage vinyl records, clothing, tools, and even furniture on eBay. The auction site earned its revenues from a small percentage taken out of every listing and another fee subtracted from each completed sale. A feedback system, in which users could report fraudulent transactions, helped keep the system honest.

Skoll and Omidyar were surprised by how quickly the eBay idea caught on. "In those early days we saw disaster around every corner," Skoll joked in an interview *New Zealand Management*. "It was quite possible that the whole thing would fall apart right away. . . . We were always mindful that at any given moment a bigger company, a Yahoo, an AOL or an Excite, could turn its attention to this space, copy what we had done, and very quickly swamp the numbers we had developed."

EBay IPO makes him a millionaire

In its first years, eBay did not even have a real street address— Skoll's home in Palo Alto served as its headquarters. He quit the Knight-Ridder job in 1996 to become eBay's full-time president, and he oversaw the company's impressive growth over the next two years. EBay's revenues grew so exponentially during its first four years that some business analysts began to claim that it was the fastest-growing company in history.

On September 24, 1998, eBay issued publicly traded shares of stock in the company on Wall Street's NASDAQ (National Association of Securities Dealers Automated Quotations) exchange. It was one of the top initial public offerings, or IPOs, of stock that year, and 218 million shares were traded that first day. Skoll was given a 7.9 percent stake in the company, with shares initially valued at $18 each. The massive media coverage of the IPO finally erased the skepticism that Skoll's family had voiced about his job. "Before then, I'd talk to my parents back in Toronto and explain what eBay was doing," he told Susanne Baillie in *Profit*. "They'd say, 'Oh, that's great. Your cousin Jerry has just started a dry cleaners!'"

Meg Whitman (1956–), a leading American corporate executive with an impressive resume, had replaced Skoll as president in the build-up to the 1998 IPO. Skoll served as eBay's vice president for strategic planning and analysis, but the long hours on the job caused back problems, and he began moving away from the daily operations at eBay. Though he was now a

The New Philanthropists

Jeff Skoll is not the only eBay executive who has turned to philanthropy. Founder Pierre Omidyar (1967–) created the Omidyar Foundation, and from that grew his Omidyar Network. The Network provides funds to such good-works projects as the Grameen Bank, which gives microloans to small business start-ups in Bangladesh, and Kids Voting USA, a youth voter-education effort in American public schools. It also gives money to non-profit organizations as well as for-profit ventures that encourage positive social change.

Skoll and Omidyar have set a good example, but they were merely following in the footsteps of others before them. The leading philanthropist of the high-tech boom is Microsoft founder Bill Gates (1955–), who set up the Bill and Melinda Gates Foundation. This is the world's largest charitable foundation, with an endowment of $28.8 billion. In 2005, it gave $750 million to the Global Alliance for Vaccines and Immunization to improve children's health around the world.

Gates's software giant created a large number of millionaires in the decade after its 1986 initial public offering, or IPO, of stock. The price of one share of Microsoft stock soared a hundredfold in its first decade of trading. Employees who had been with Microsoft in its early days, and received stock options as part of their benefits packages, were millionaires by the mid-1990s. Some of them cashed out that stock and began venturing into philanthropy. One such "Microsoft millionaire" was Stephanie DeVaan, who founded a political action committee in Washington, D.C, called Washington Women for Choice. Another, John Sage, founded Pura Vida, an organic coffee supplier.

millionaire, he still lived in his modest home in Palo Alto and drove the same car he had in college. But he became increasingly interested in sharing his wealth. Even before eBay's IPO, he had convinced other executives to set up the eBay Foundation, a charitable fund created to give back to the community, with pre-IPO shares. When the Foundation's 105,000 shares of stock began trading on the NASDAQ, the earnings from it funded various charitable projects, such as homeless shelters in the Bay Area.

Funds several charitable ventures

In 1999, Skoll began giving away some of his own money. His donations included the largest amount ever given to a Canadian university by someone under the age of forty. He gave the money to his alma mater, the University of Toronto, to create a joint engineering/business degree program. He also donated a sum to

Stanford University for its Center for Electronic Business and Commerce and became increasingly active in the Community Foundation Silicon Valley (CFSV). This umbrella organization provided grants and funds to several local charities and social-service agencies operating in the southern part of the Bay area known as Silicon Valley. This corridor of communities, anchored by the city of San Jose, is the center of the U.S. high-tech industry, and its industrial parks are home to the headquarters of such companies as Apple Computer, Hewlett-Packard, and Sun Microsystems.

In June 1999, Skoll set up his Skoll Community Fund to specifically fund the CFSV's work, and he also encouraged others to join him in giving back to the community. Since the Internet era had begun in the mid-1990s, there hadbeen an immense number of new millionaires created among Silicon Valley executives when their companies became publicly traded ones. Skoll began meeting with them and urging the new "dotcom millionaires," as the media called them, to become philanthropists, too, by donating "to a cause they cared about," he told Watson in *Canadian Business*. "You know, they have millions and millions of shares, and if they give away a hundred thousand shares, they're not gonna miss it. But if the stock goes away, at least they will have done something good."

Skoll also launched the Skoll Foundation in 1999. Its aim was to further the idea of social entrepreneurship, or combining the profit-centered focus of business management with the idea of improving the lives of the planet's neediest citizens. As he knew from his eBay experience, an idea that personally changed people's lives could also have immense profit potential. Many people who had otherwise been shut out of the traditional economy, such as stay-at-home mothers, disabled people, and senior citizens, had found on eBay a way to earn extra or even primary income, and many reported that they had found a tremendous sense of accomplishment as well. Social entrepreneurship expanded that idea further. Finding ways to help underdeveloped countries prosper was one way. "Right now, about half the world lives on less than $1 a day," Skoll explained to Jeffrey

Gangemi in *Business Week Online*. "Social entrepreneurship offers a way to get to that half of humanity that isn't attractive to traditional big businesses and bring them up the ladder."

Establishes Oxford University program

Skoll's commitment to the principles of social entrepreneurship was demonstrated with the establishment of the Skoll Center for Social Entrepreneurship at Oxford University in England. The Center was part of Oxford's Said Business School, founded by Syrian-born entrepreneur Wafic Saïd (1939–), who made a fortune in construction in Saudi Arabia in the 1970s during its oil-boom years. One example of work done there was a project created to improve land that is not arable, or able to grow crops, by planting a fast-growing weed that fertilizes the soil. The weed, in turn, can be harvested and made into diesel fuel. The process requires a fair amount of labor, but such projects are a suitable match for parts of Africa and the Third World where people are plenty but jobs are scarce.

Skoll also became one of Hollywood's unlikeliest new film moguls when he established Participant Productions, a film-production company, with actor, director, and producer Robert Redford (1937–). Its mission, Skoll told the press, was to make feature films and documentaries with a social message. Its first project was *Syriana,* a political thriller centered around international oil espionage starring Matt Damon (1970–) and George Clooney (1961–). The work was slated for a November 2005 theater release. Another work funded by Participant Productions was *American Gun*, a feature film about gun violence and its effect on the lives of several individuals. Skoll's film company hoped to finance a half-dozen similar projects every year and would put up the first $20 million or so; a major studio—like Warner Bros. Pictures, which helped finance the making of *Syriana*—would contribute the rest. "It helps that I'm able to bring some of the financing, because it takes some of the risk out of the equation for the studio," Skoll told *Fortune* journalist Adam Lashinsky. "People genuinely want to make films they can be proud of."

Skoll views his philanthropy as a logical extension of his business ideas. There was, he told Della Bradshaw of the *Financial Times,* "a great social element to eBay. We think the heart and the wallet go very well together." He explained his philosophy further to *Business Week Online.* "Any individual can make a difference," he asserted. "Business skills, when well applied, can do more than just make money. They can potentially make money and do some real good, which is immensely satisfying."

For More Information

Periodicals

Antonucci, Mike. "Uncommon Partnership Yields Film for the Common Good." *San Jose Mercury News* (June 24, 2005).

Baillie, Susanne. "High Tech Heroes." *Profit* (December 2000/January 2001).

Bick, Julie. "The Microsoft Millionaires." *New York Times* (May 29, 2005): p. B5.

Bradshaw, Della. "An Impetus for Social Change." *Financial Times* (December 1, 2003): p. 12.

Dearlove, Des. "EBay's Jeff Skoll on Business' Social Revolution." *New Zealand Management* (April 2004): p. 34.

Dearlove, Des, and Peter Brown. "It Just Seemed Like the World Was Headed Down a Scary Path—And I Wanted to Do Something about It." *Times* (London, England) (January 26, 2004): p. 6.

Lashinsky, Adam. "Ebay's First Hire Goes to the Movies." *Fortune* (March 7, 2005): p. 36.

Omidyar, Pierre. "The Idea Man: Jeff Skoll." *Time International* (January 27, 2003): p. 48.

Web Sites

"An Entrepreneur Who Cares." *Business Week Online.* http://www.businessweek.com/bschools/content/jun2005/bs20050616_5577_bs001.htm (accessed on August 23, 2005).

Skoll Foundation. http://www.skollfoundation.org (accessed on August 23, 2005).

Watson, Thomas. "Live and Learn." *Canadian Business 75th Anniversary Special.* http://www.canadianbusiness75.com/profile2.htm (accessed on August 23, 2005).

Joss Stone

April 11, 1987 • *Dover, England*

Singer

Teen singing sensation Joss Stone came out of nowhere to take the music industry by storm. The British blues singer grew up listening to American music as well as several other genres. In fact, she landed her first record contract by singing a cover version of disco queen Donna Summer's 1970s hit "On the Radio." Two albums and several Top 20 singles later, Stone is being hailed by some as the white Aretha Franklin (1942–), a woman who is considered one of the best rhythm and blues singers of all time.

A poor student, a talented singer

Joscelyn Eve Stoker was born on April 11, 1987, in Dover, England. She moved with her three siblings and parents to Ashill, a small town where Stone spent most of her childhood; this is where she began to dislike school. Stone is dyslexic, which means she sometimes sees and reads things backwards or mixed up. But this isn't the only reason she grew to dread school every morning. "It was partly that, but because I don't come across like I'm really stupid—I can hold a conversation. . . . I guess teachers thought I wasn't trying. . . ." Stone explained to Teddy Jamieson of *The Herald*. "The way they taught didn't work, so that resulted in huge arguments with people and I don't like to be told what to do."

So Stone spent a fair amount of her time in detention, figuring if that was the worst thing that could happen to her, she'd survive. And still she found time to shape her musical

"I just think my voice is suited to a time that doesn't exist anymore."

tastes. Stone's father listened to blues and reggae for the most part. Her mother's tastes lay in soul music. Soul is a sound that emerged in the late 1950s and early 1960s. It is an offshoot of the sounds of rock and roll and gospel. Soul is divided into several categories, including Motown (sung by African Americans on the Motown record label) and blue-eyed soul (performed by white musicians). Musicians such as James Brown (1928–) added their own style to soul and took it in another direction. Brown is credited with helping to make the funk sound popular in the 1960s.

Stone grew up listening to the great soul musicians from the past, and by the time she was seven years old, Aretha Franklin was her hero. Franklin, whose roots were in gospel, earned herself the title "Queen of Soul" with timeless hits such as "Respect" and "Chain of Fools." The first woman to be inducted into the Rock and Roll Hall of Fame, Franklin began recording gospel at the age of fourteen. She was still generating hits in the pop music genre in the 1970s and 1980s. Franklin is considered one of the greatest crossover (spanning more than one genre) music recording stars in history. *Aretha Franklin's Greatest Hits* was the first album Stone owned, and she spent much of her free time listening and singing along. Stone found her voice well-suited to the throaty sounds of the blues. One day she would amaze listeners with a powerful sound that didn't seem like it could come from a girl who was not yet out of her teens.

At age twelve, Stone chose to become a singer by default. In her interview with *The Herald,* she explained that she thought she might like to become a veterinarian or midwife (a nurse who is licensed to deliver babies). "But then I realized that meant seven years at school. I couldn't do that so I decided to be a singer." Most children dream of being a famous musician at some point. For Stone, that dream came true without so much as one day of struggle.

High school dropout makes it big

Stone was thirteen when she submitted an audition tape to the British talent show *Star for a Night.* Her cover of the Aretha Franklin hit "(You Make Me Feel Like) a Natural Woman" won her a spot on the show. Onstage and live on television, Stone's rendition of Donna Summer's "On the Radio" left the audience speechless. This blonde, giggly teenager had the voice of a grown woman. She immediately signed on with American record company executive Steve Greenberg of S-Curve Records. Greenberg is credited with bringing the pop group Hanson to the masses.

Greenberg recognized Stone's potential and hired Miami soul legend Betty Wright to mentor Stone. Wright began singing when her own mother suffered a back injury and could no longer support her fatherless family. In a 2003 interview with Scott Simon of National Public Radio (NPR), Wright explained the difference between her early years as a star and Stone's. "I think in Joss's case, there's a lot more fun involved, and I'm really glad for that. Mine eventually became that.... I think it's very stressful, in my case because I had not just, you know, singing for soup, but it was like I have a big family, so it was like no matter how much money you bring home, sometimes it's not enough."

Stone considers Wright to be her second "mum," (mom) and the two joke about how Wright threatens Stone with guitar sticks if she doesn't stay on track. Stone's mother was actually her manager in the beginning. When rumors started circulating that Stone fired her mother, the singer scoffed. As she explained to Teddy Jamieson of *The Herald,* "She was my mum and she managed me for a little second, but at the end of the day at some point you can't take your mum to work with you. That's pretty much all it is."

Stone dropped out of school at sixteen, with her parents' approval. In an interview with *SMH.com,* the singer remembered, "I was never an academic sort of kid. My parents knew I hated school and I really just looked forward to leaving." When it became obvious Stone's career was going to take her in the right direction, her parents gave her their blessing. With a voice that Wright calls "a gift from heaven," it seemed silly to make the singer continue along a path that wasn't taking her where she wanted to go.

Around this time, the singer decided to change her name, though she did so reluctantly. Her mom thought she needed something catchier than Stoker. In the end, Stone changed it to protect her family from the media attention, since her grandmother had the same last name.

The Soul Sessions

Wright gathered a team of musicians to create what she calls a Miami soul sound. It's a sound of mixed cultures—reggae, calypso, salsa, and blues. These musicians backed up sixteen-year-old Stone on her debut album, *The Soul Sessions.* Released on September 16, 2003, the album is a treasure trove of classic soul tracks, remade the Stone way. It reached the Top 5 in the U.K. charts, the Top 100 in the U.S. Billboard charts.

A couple singles from the album fared especially well. "Fell in Love with a Boy" was a cover of alternative rock group The White Stripes's song "Fell in Love with a Girl." Stone's version reached the Top 20 in the U.K.'s singles chart. "Super Duper Love (Are You Diggin' On Me?)" enjoyed the same success.

Stone expressed her uncertainty at working with a crew of powerhouse musicians in an interview with *MTV News.* "I felt a

At the 47th Grammy Awards, Melissa Etheridge and Joss Stone brought the audience to its feet during their tribute to the late Janis Joplin. AP/Wide World Photos.

bit weird about the whole thing because 'Should I be here?' I have no experience, I don't know what I'm doing. But it was cool because they made me feel really comfortable." By the summer of 2004 *The Soul Sessions* was certified gold in the United States and had sold more than two million copies worldwide.

Mind, Body & Soul

Stone performed on television shows such as *Good Morning, America* and *The Conan O'Brien Show* following the release of her first album. She could boast that among her fans were actor Tom Cruise and rock and roll legend Mick Jagger. She appeared in *Rolling Stone* and *People* magazines. She was hot. But she wasn't about to stop there.

In an article on her U.K. Web site, Stone admits that *The Soul Sessions* "started out as a side project and turned into this huge thing. I didn't mean it to, but people just kept buying it." A little less than a year later, Stone released her sophomore album, *Mind, Body & Soul*. "For me, personally, *Mind, Body & Soul* is my real debut," Stone explains on her Web site. Released in the United States on September 28, 2004, the album contained mostly original songs. Stone cowrote eleven of the fourteen tunes.

"I think my singing is so much better on this album. Your voice can't ever be the same, once you've started singing live as much as I have over the past year," says the singer on her Web site. Many of the songs were recorded in chunks because Stone was touring and playing gigs during the production of the album. Despite that, the sound is not overproduced. Listeners would never know it was pieced together in the studio. The album reached number eleven on Billboard's Top 200 chart in 2004. In October of that year, the album reached number one in the United Kingdom. *Mind, Body & Soul* also went certified gold in the United States.

2005: A year of making lists

Every year, the United Kingdom hosts the Brit Awards. These awards are given to musicians in a number of categories. Stone was nominated in three categories in 2005 and won two of them. She was voted Best Female British Solo Artist and Best British Urban Act. Stone was just seventeen years old.

In 2005 Stone also was added to the list of Britain's young music millionaires. To qualify for the list, musicians must be thirty years old or younger. Stone, at seventeen, entered at number fourteen with earnings over $5 million. This amount was expected to rise with the continued sale of *Mind, Body & Soul*.

Perhaps the highest praise Stone could have received in 2005 was to be nominated for three Grammy Awards, including Best New Artist. Though she did not win, the blues singer did get to sing a live duet with famous rocker Melissa Etheridge (1961–) at the Grammy show in February 2005. The two dedicated their medley to the late great rocker Janis Joplin (1943–1970), and it instantly became the number-one download on the iTunes Web site. All proceeds went toward breast cancer research. (Etheridge had recently undergone surgery for breast cancer.)

Stone was officially recognized as the hip, classy up-and-comer when she became the spokesperson for the Gap store's summer campaign of 2005. She became not only the face, but also the sound of Gap. Stone's music was used in Gap ads beginning in April of that year. For the fall campaign, Stone joined recording stars such as Alanis Morissette and Liz Phair to compile a promotional CD for the Gap. Stone sang the Beach Boys's hit "God Only Knows" for that CD, which was released in September 2005.

Plays concerts in the park

In July 2005, Stone was one of more than one thousand musicians to donate their time and talent to participate in Live 8, a concert held in ten cities across the globe. Its mission was to raise awareness of poverty in Africa. Stone performed in London with a list of legendary musicians including Madonna, U2, Coldplay, Dido, Pink Floyd, and the Dave Matthews Band. Stone entertained millions of viewers with the songs "Some Kind of Wonderful" and "Super Duper Love."

According to *Contactmusic.com,* Stone was so nervous before going on stage that she became violently ill. "I just get so worried about seeing such a massive crowd and not being able to hack it," the tall crooner is quoted as saying.

Just days after performing at Live 8, Stone showed up on stage at T in the Park, Scotland's largest music festival. A ticket to the festival brought you about one hundred musical performances over a period of two days. Stone was among many popular bands, including Foo Fighters, Jimmy Eat World, Snoop Dogg, and Audioslave. T in the Park is a phenomenally popular event. Twenty-five thousand tickets for the 2006 show sold out in three hours.

Stone and her boyfriend, Beau Dozier, live in Encino, California. Dozier, who is eight years older than Stone, is also

Live 8 Brings Together Politics and Food

In 1985, more than one hundred musicians performed at concerts held in Europe and the United States. The event was called Live Aid. More than 162,000 people attended the concerts, with an estimated 1.5 billion viewers tuning in to television broadcasts. Live Aid raised $200 million for famine relief in Ethiopia. The event was an amazing collaboration of celebrities and organizers, the chief being Irish rocker Bob Geldof (1951–).

Twenty years later, in July 2005, Geldof once again pulled off a spectacular feat: More than one thousand artists performed in four continents and ten cities. They were not paid one penny for their time or travel expenses. In total, $25 billion was pledged to Africa by the eight wealthiest nations in the world. This money would go directly to fight poverty and improve health care in Africa. Frontman Bono, of the famous band U2, put it this way in an article at *Star-eCentral.com*: "Live Aid raised $250 million (in 1985) and we were cock-a-hoop [thrilled]. But this is $25 billion for Africa and that's new money. . . . The world spoke, and the politicians listened."

According to the Live 8 Web site, more than one million people attended the concerts on July 2, while another two billion watched and listened via television. Tickets for the performances were free. Live 8 was held in conjunction with the G8 Summit. The Summit involved the eight most powerful nations (group of eight: France, Germany, Italy, Japan, the United States, the United Kingdom, Canada, and Russia) in the world, and they gathered in Britain to discuss how to help fight the alarming level of poverty in Africa. British prime minister Tony Blair (1953–) credited Live

8 with helping to make the G8 summit a "mighty achievement." By the time the summit ended, summit members had pledged an additional $25 billion in aid, bringing the total pledge to $50 billion. They also cancelled the debts of the eighteen poorest countries and committed to training twenty thousand peacekeepers for African American leaders to use to help usher in democracy.

Geldof initially did not want to plan Live 8. He explained his feelings to Pete Norman of *People*: "I'm loath to mess with Live Aid. It was a perfect day. . . ." Geldof was approached by his old friend Bono to organize a new and improved event. After much arguing, Bono convinced Geldof that another concert event could work. Geldof told *BBC News,* "In 1985 it was about charity, raising money for charity, when it was Live Aid. Today it's about a campaign for justice and empowerment for millions of people around the world. . . ."

At the time of the G8 Summit and Live 8, 51 percent of Africans were under the age of fifteen. About 1.9 million children were infected with the HIV virus (the virus that leads to the deadly AIDS disease), and 17 million Africans had already died from AIDS. AIDS stands for Auto-Immune Deficiency Syndrome. It is a disease that weakens the immune system, making the body more susceptible to many illnesses, and eventually kills its victims. According to Bono's *DATA* Web site, 6,300 Africans die every day fromAIDS or HIV infection. More than 300 million people—nearly half the population—of Sub-Saharan Africa live on $1 a day. But the country spends $30 billion a year repaying debts to the richest countries in the world.

her record producer. The two met when he helped produce her *Mind, Body, & Soul* album.

Looking ahead

Stone planned to hit the recording studio with British pal Sir Elton John (1947–) to release a Christmas duet in 2005. Stone thought about another album during an interview published on *EdmuntonSun.com*: "I have so many ideas. Maybe I'll go a little funky, maybe I won't. Maybe I'll record it like this, maybe I won't. I'm not really sure. It'll be a nice surprise."

For More Information

Periodicals

Graham, Caroline. "Will Joss Stone's under-age love affair cost her the millions?" *Daily Mail* (April 3, 2005).

Norman, Pete. "Greatest Show on Earth: Backed by his stellar speed-dial and the historic success of Live Aid, Bob Geldof put together the sequel, Live 8." *People* (July 11, 2005).

Web Sites

Debt AIDS Trade Africa (DATA). http://www.data.org (accessed on August 8, 2005).

"Devon's young pop millionaires." *BBC* (April 1, 2005). http://www.bbc.co.uk/devon/music/2005/04_april/music_millionaires.shtml (accessed on August 8, 2005).

Jamieson, Teddy. "Is Joss Stone big enough now to be her own boss?" *The Herald* (July 11, 2005). http://www.theherald.co.uk/features/42676.html (accessed on August 8, 2005).

"Joss and Muse do Devon proud at Brits." *BBC*. http://www.bbc.co.uk/devon/music/2005/brits.shtml (accessed on August 8, 2005).

Joss Stone. http://www.jossstone.co.uk/ (accessed on August 8, 2005).

"Joss Stone: Biography." *VH1.com*. http://www.vh1.com/artists/az/stone_joss/bio.jhtml (accessed on August 8, 2005).

Live 8. http://www.live8live.com (accessed on August 8, 2005).

"Live 8 helped aid deal says Blair." *BBC News* (July 11, 2005). http://newsvote.bbc.co.uk/go/pr/fr/-/1/hi/uk_politics/4672797.stm (accessed August 8, 2005).

"Live 8 success hailed by Geldof." *BBC News* (July 3, 2005). http://news.bbc.co.uk/go/pr/fr/-/1/hi/entertainment/music/4645823.stm (accessed on August 8, 2005).

Rocca, Jane. "A pretty blonde with black soul." *SMH.com*
(March 1, 2004). http://www.smh.com.au/articles/2004/03/01/
1077989486224.html (accessed on August 8, 2005).

Audio

Simon, Scott. "Interview: Joss Stone and Betty Wright discuss Stone's
singing career." *NPR: Weekend Edition* (September 13, 2003).

Ichiro Suzuki

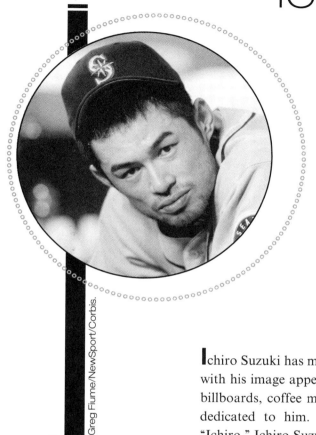

October 22, 1973 • *Kasugai, Japan*

Baseball player

Ichiro Suzuki has millions of dedicated fans in his native Japan, with his image appearing in daily newspapers and smiling from billboards, coffee mugs, and T-shirts. There is even a museum dedicated to him. Known to his adoring public simply as "Ichiro," Ichiro Suzuki is more than just a baseball player; he is a national institution. Considered by many to be the greatest hitter in Japanese baseball history, Ichiro dominated the game in his homeland for nearly nine years until he was snapped up in 2001 to play professional baseball for the American League's Seattle Mariners. As a result, he became the first Japanese position player (meaning a nonpitcher) to be signed by a U.S. team. Since then the fleet-footed, left-handed outfielder has broken dozens of records and has garnered an enormous American following. In 2004, Ichiro had his hottest streak ever, finishing the year by breaking a record that had stood untouched for eighty-four years: scoring the most hits in a single season. He is called a "hitting machine" by sportswriters. This is no exaggeration, since according to Leigh Montville of *Sports Illustrated*, "Any pitch, any time, any place, any situation—you throw it, Ichiro will hit it."

First boy makes good

Ichiro Suzuki was born on October 22, 1973, in Kasugai, Japan. Ichiro's father, Nobuyuki, was determined that Ichiro, who he thought had a natural talent for baseball, would play the sport, and play it well. The elder Suzuki made it clear from the begin-

> "I'm unique. I'm a very rare kind of player."

ning that his son was special. In fact, the name Ichiro means "first boy," even though he was actually the second boy born to the family. From the time he was three years old, Ichiro was practicing in his backyard with a tiny bat and ball, and by elementary school, Nobuyuki, who was a former high school ballplayer himself, was putting his son through batting drills for up to four hours per day.

In high school Ichiro already displayed a dedication to the game that he would become known for as an adult. It was a tradition at Nagoya Electric High School that freshman players were responsible for washing the uniforms of the seniors, so to make sure he had plenty of time for practice Ichiro would get up at 3:00 AM to do laundry. The young batter also maintained a rigorous class schedule and excelled academically. By his senior year Ichiro was a familiar face at Japan's National High School Baseball Tournament, known as *Koshien*. Upon graduation from high school in 1991, he was drafted to play professional ball for the Pacific League's BlueWave, a team owned by the Japanese leasing company Orix.

During his first year with the BlueWave, Ichiro devoted himself to perfecting his game. As S. L. Price of *Sports Illustrated* commented, "He spent most of his free time in the batting cage, with teammates coming and going from breakfast, lunch, nap, dinner to the endless tattoo of his bat on ball." Ichiro also developed a very unique batting stance that included lifting his right leg and swinging it back and forth like a pendulum. His hours of practice proved to be worth it; Ichiro quickly became known as a slasher at the plate, hitting line drives to the corners of every ballpark in every game.

During his seven full seasons playing for the BlueWave, the left-handed hitter racked up an impressive record: Each season he hit between .342 and .387 and averaged twenty-nine doubles, seventeen home runs, and twenty-eight stolen bases. He also earned seven batting titles and set a national record for getting to first base in fifty-seven consecutive games. Ichiro was named Most Valuable Player three times, and in 1998 he was key to leading the BlueWave to their first Pacific League pennant.

National icon

Ichiro's prowess in the batting box quickly helped make him the most well-known and celebrated person in Japan, but it was his style that catapulted him to mythic proportions. With a lean, teenager-like physique, spiky hair, and a penchant for wearing sunglasses and his baseball cap backwards, the five-foot-nine Ichiro was not the typical, conservative Japanese player. He especially appealed to younger fans, who viewed him as something of a rock star. Ichiro soon became a one-man industry, with his own line of sports apparel, including colorful Nike Air Max sneakers that were snatched up by the millions.

Another suggested reason for Ichiro's popularity was his notoriety for being tight-lipped in interviews. "He is a man of few words, so he doesn't talk so much," noted Michael Knisley of *Sporting News*. "And the more mysterious he acts, the more mystique he has." According to Jeff Pearlman of *Sports Illustrated,* the reason for Ichiro's reserve was more practical: If he thinks he has not contributed to a game he feels there is simply nothing to say. The fashionably dressed hitter may have been aloof with the press, but he obviously enjoyed playing to, and sometimes with, the crowd. In fact, during game lulls Ichiro was known to play catch with fans sitting in the right-field stands.

Ichiro reached the pinnacle of fame when, in 2000, his father built a four-story museum in Nagoya, Japan, dedicated solely to his celebrated son. Nearly three thousand articles are on display chronicling the life and times of Ichiro, which is amazing considering he was only twenty-four when the museum opened. Items include his childhood Nintendo game cartridges, baseball jerseys, report cards, nearly one hundred scrapbooks containing news clippings—and even Ichiro's dental retainer. According to the museum manager, who spoke with Jim Caple of *ESPN.com,* "When Ichiro was a child his father told Ichiro's mother, 'He is going to be a great athlete. We must keep everything.'"

Ichiro conquers America

Although he was a star in Japan, Ichiro had been setting his sights on American baseball since the spring of 1999, when he spent two weeks in spring training with the Seattle Mariners. In 2000 he announced to Orix that once his full nine years playing pro ball in Japan was up, which it would be in 2001, he was going to consider offers from other teams, including those from the United States. Aware that Ichiro's departure was unavoidable, and faced with business losses, Orix decided to "post" Ichiro, meaning they put Ichiro on the auction block. The Mariners beat out other hopeful franchises, and on November 9, 2000, offered Orix more than $13 million for a thirty-day window to negotiate with Ichiro. On November 18, the powerhouse hitter signed a three-year deal with Seattle worth a reported $15-$20 million. He became the first Japanese position player to sign with a U.S. baseball team.

Ichiro may have been eager to play American ball, but he claimed the decision to leave Japan was a hard one. "I never said it was easy for me," he revealed to John Rawlings of *Sporting News.* "But it wasn't interesting anymore. People have twisted that very often. As the better pitchers left my league, it wasn't fun." Ichiro also claimed to be both hesitant and excited about his move. As he told Michael Farber of *Sports Illustrated,* "Sometimes I am nervous, sometimes anxious, but I want to challenge a new world." Ichiro began to adapt to his new life by asking in his contract for English lessons for himself and his wife,

Japanese television personality Yumiko Fukushima. He also made it clear that, just as he had in Japan, he wanted to be recognized by his first name only. In May 2001 Ichiro became the first and only U.S. player to wear a baseball jersey bearing only a first name.

The Mariners did not regret opening their purse for their Japanese import. By the end of his first season Ichiro was known, according to Rick Reilly, as "the fastest man in baseball with the best outfield arm playing for the winningest team." He posted a .357 batting average, with fifty-six stolen bases, leading the major leagues in both categories. Ichiro also became only the second player to be voted American League Rookie of the Year and Most Valuable Player in the same season. Over the next three years the Japanese slugger continued to be the most successful and consistent leadoff hitter in U.S. baseball. "I don't think you can pitch him one way," New York Yankees's manager Joe Torre commented to Jeff Pearlman. "You can go in and out, up and down and he makes the adjustment. You can get ahead of the count, and Ichiro still seems relaxed. He doesn't seem to have any weaknesses."

Ichiro's clear focus and intense concentration contributed to such comments, and his many rituals clearly intrigued American fans and members of the press. Sportswriters reported on his exercise regimen, which included a constant stretching and rolling of shoulders when he is in the outfield between pitches; a massage before each game; and methodically rubbing his feet with a wooden stick in the locker room. According to Ichiro, and according to Eastern medicine, healthy feet are key to a healthy body. A wooden stick helps massage certain points on the foot that supposedly improve such things as flexibility and circulation.

Ichiro also believes that mental preparation is equally important to physical preparation. Before each game he watches a tape of his opposing pitchers, and after each game he spends time by himself with only his handcrafted glove for company. Ichiro carefully wipes away any dirt from the glove, rubs in a protective cream, and checks all the lacings. As he explained to Brad Lefton of *Sporting News,* "The glove is directly connected to

Out of the Shadows: George Sisler

When Ichiro Suzuki hit his way into sports history he also put the spotlight on another player who had almost been forgotten in the shadows: George Sisler. Sisler is considered by many to be one of the greatest first basemen of all time and perhaps the most legendary player in the history of the St. Louis Browns. He had a fifteen-year batting average of .340; he was a swift base runner; and he was known for his acrobatic fielding. But Sisler was also a quiet and modest man whose reputation was eclipsed by some of his more charismatic contemporaries such as Ty Cobb (1886–1961) and Babe Ruth (1895–1948).

George Harold Sisler was born on March 24, 1893, in Manchester, Ohio, but spent his early years in Nimisila, a tiny coal-mining town just south of Akron. From early on, baseball was his life. When he was fourteen Sisler moved to Akron in order to pitch for Akron Central High School. While still in high school he signed a contract to play professional ball, which would take effect as soon as he graduated. Sisler's father, however, urged him to pursue his education first, so in 1910 he enrolled at the University of Michigan (U of M) in Ann Arbor. During his years at U of M Sisler emerged as one of the top college ballplayers in the country, and although he graduated in 1915 with a degree in mechanical engineering he decided to turn pro, signing with the American League's St. Louis Browns.

Sisler began his career as a pitcher, but because he was too good with a bat to be limited to hitting once every four days, he soon took over at first base. From 1915 until 1922 Sisler maintained a .374 batting average, reaching .407 in 1920 and peaking at .420 in 1922, a record that no one has since approached. "Gorgeous George," as he was known to his fans, continued to rack up record after record, and in 1920 he was at the pinnacle of his career, reaching the single-season record of 257 hits that remained untouched until 2004. Sisler also achieved career bests of 19 home runs, 18 triples, 49 doubles, 122 runs batted in, and 137 runs scored. According to sports historian Bill James, who spoke with Dave Kindred of *Sporting News,* in 1920 Sisler was "about as great of a player as you can be."

Unfortunately the baseball legend's career was cut short in 1923 after he suffered a bout of sinusitis

the game. There's a special meaning in reflecting back on your day's work while paying homage to a piece of equipment that helped you. So while I care for my glove, I also reflect back on my mistakes and try to identify the causes."

Sizzles Sisler's record

Mistakes did not come often for Ichiro, although he did experience a bit of a slump in 2003, when he finished the year with a disappointing-for-him .257 average. A refreshed Ichiro, however, was back in action in 2004, and as the season progressed he broke record after record. Nicknamed Wizard by his (a severe sinus infection), which caused double vision for a time and forced him to sit out the entire season. Sisler continued to play for the Browns until 1928, when he was traded to the Washington Senators. After appearing in only twenty games Washington turned his contract over to the Boston Braves, who kept Sisler on the roster until 1930. Although he performed admirably, Sisler never quite achieved his former glory, and he considered 1923 to be his last true year in baseball. After playing briefly in the minor leagues for two years Sisler retired in 1932. He left professional baseball for the next ten years, but returned to the major leagues in 1943 to scout for the Brooklyn Dodgers. From 1951 through 1965 Sisler served as a scout and hitting instructor for the Pittsburgh Pirates. He died on March 26, 1973, at the age of eighty.

Two of Sisler's sons, Dick and Dave, played major league ball in the 1950s, and a third son, George Jr., served as an executive in the minor leagues. Five members of the Sisler family were on hand when Ichiro Suzuki broke Gorgeous George's eighty-four-year-old record. As Sisler's grandson, Bo Drochelman, told Bob Sherwin of the *Seattle Times,* "My grandfather really respected the game of baseball. He cherished it and played every minute to the hilt.

George Sisler. AP/Wide World Photos.

That's the part of Ichiro I think he would have loved, a man dedicated to the game. That would have made him proud, that kind of person breaking his record."

teammates he proved he had magic in his feet, his glove, and especially his bat. Ichiro became one of only eleven players to have four consecutive 200-hit seasons, and as the playoffs drew closer speculations were flying that he would beat the single-season hitting record of 257 set in 1920 by George Sisler (1893–1973) of the St. Louis Browns.

On October 1, 2004, before a sold-out crowd, Ichiro tied the record during the first inning of the Mariners-Texas Rangers game. During the third inning he rocketed a line drive to left field and secured his place in baseball history. The stands erupted; fireworks soared over the ballpark; and teammates and fans gave Ichiro a two-minute standing ovation as he

Ichiro Suzuki scrambles back to first base during the fourth inning of the 2005 Major League Baseball All-Star Game. AP/Wide World Photos.

stood, beaming, on first base. "It's definitely the most emotional I have gotten in my life," the usually calm and collected Ichiro admitted to Bob Sherwin of the *Seattle Times* after the game. "It's definitely the highlight of my career, and I was thinking 'Is there something better in my future?'"

Considering he was only thirty years old when he broke Sisler's record, many predicted that there was much more ahead in Ichiro's future. By mid-2005 he had already broken at least two more batting records: On June 14 he became only the third major league player in history to hit one thousand runs in less than seven hundred games; and on July 30 Ichiro reached his 1,058th hit, the most any player has achieved in their first five-seasons of play. Don Baylor, the hitting coach for the Mariners, forecast that his star right-fielder would possibly break an unprecedented .400 batting average by season's end if he started the year at .350; as of July 2005 Ichiro was batting .385. The modest Mariner, as usual, was cautious when speaking to the press about the hype. As he told Phil Rogers of *ChicagoSports.com,* "I don't know if I'll ever do it. I just want to be a player people say has a chance." For a man who S. L. Price claims has become an "an omnipresent cultural icon," that is definitely an understatement.

For More Information

Periodicals

Farber, Michael. "Rising Son: The Defection of Ichiro Suzuki." *Sports Illustrated* (December 4, 2000): p. 68.

Kindred, Dave. "Ichiro Is a Vision of Hitters Past." *The Sporting News* (October 4, 2004): p. 64.

Knisley, Michael. "Follow That Star!" *The Sporting News* (March 19, 2001): p. 12.

Lefton, Brad. "In Focus: Mariners Outfielder Ichiro Suzuki's Mental Preparation Is as Big a Part of His Game as His Blazing Speed and Powerful Throwing Arm." *The Sporting News* (March 10, 2003): pp. 10–14.

Montville, Leigh. "The Single Guy: Ichiro Suzuki." *Sports Illustrated* (October 4, 2004): p. 20.

Pearlman, Jeff. "Big Hit: Ichiro Suzuki." *Sports Illustrated* (May 28, 2001): p. 34.

Price, S. L. "The Ichiro Paradox." *Sports Illustrated* (July 8, 2002): p. 50.

Rawlings, John. "A Star Arrives." *The Sporting News* (March 19, 2001): p. 6.

Reilly, Rick. "Itching for Ichiro." *Sports Illustrated* (September 17, 2001): p. 112.

Verducci, Tom. "Leading Man: The Job of the Leadoff Hitter Is to Get on Base, and Who Does It Better than Ichiro Suzuki?" *Sports Illustrated* (April 4, 2005): p. 58.

Web Sites

Caple, Jim. "It's All Ichiro All the Time at the Ichiro Exhibition Room." *ESPN.com: Baseball* (November 14, 2002). http://espn.go.com/mlb/columns/caple_jim/1460455.html (accessed on August 23, 2005).

Sherwin, Bob. "Hits-tory! Ichiro Breaks Sisler's Record." *The Seattle Times* (October 2, 2004). http://seattletimes.nwsource.com/html/mariners/2002052125_ichiroheads02.html (accessed on August 23, 2005).

.

Kanye West

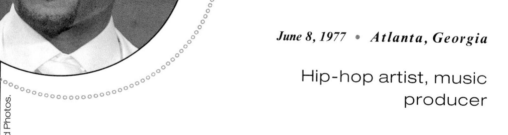

AP/Wide World Photos.

June 8, 1977 • *Atlanta, Georgia*

Hip-hop artist, music producer

Kanye West is a quadruple threat: producer, rapper, songwriter, and record executive. His albums have sold millions; his lyrics are sung by renowned recording artists including Brandy, Usher, and Alicia Keys. In 2005, West was named to *Time* magazine's list of One Hundred Most Influential People in the World. He was in good company, with a peer group that included talk show host Oprah Winfrey (1954–), actor **Jamie Foxx** (1967–; see entry), and actor Clint Eastwood (1930–). West's lyrics have been criticized for encouraging children and young adults to drop out of school, an allegation he claims is based on a misunderstanding. His newest album, *Late Registration,* was released in August 2005.

Southern born, Chicago raised

Kanye (Swahili [African] for "only one") West was born in Atlanta, Georgia, on June 8, 1977. His parents divorced when

West was three. He was raised on Chicago's South Side by his mother, an English professor, and spent summers with his father, an award-winning photographer who became a church counselor.

West graduated from Polaris High School and completed one year of art school at Chicago State University. He explained his decision to drop out of school to Kimberly Davis in a 2004 interview with *Ebony* magazine. "I dropped out of school because I wasn't learning fast enough.... I learned from real life better." Real life at that time included rapping and working with local artists. West felt it was time to pursue his music career full time,

> " My [future] is in God's hands. If He wants me to make another album, then He'll give me the inspiration to do so. I can't force it. "

so he moved to New York in 2001. His mixes and beats were getting him a reputation as a man who knew his jams. Respected rapper Jay-Z (1969–) hired him to produce songs for his 2001 album *The Blueprint*. Sales of that album exceeded 420,000 in the first week alone. West went on to produce for a handful of stars including rapper Ludacris and singer Beyonce. He was doing well, making a name for himself. But he wanted more.

Releases *College Dropout*

While acting as producer to the stars, West cut his own demo (a recording that gives listeners an idea of the style and ability of the musician) and began shopping it around. Despite his solid reputation, no one returned his calls. Then in 2002, Roc-A-Fella Records, the label that signed Jay-Z, decided to give West a chance as a rapper. The company already knew he was a talented record producer. West signed a record deal that year and began recording in the studio.

On the way home from a recording session in Los Angeles, West fell asleep at the wheel and was involved in a head-on car collision that left him with a broken face and fractured jaw. The artist nearly died in the crash. He endured months of recovery, including reconstructive surgery that left his jaw wired shut. That didn't stop West from moving forward with the album. He explained the ordeal to *Ebony* magazine: "I feel like the album was my medicine. It would take my mind away from the pain—away from the dental appointments, from my teeth killing me, from my mouth being wired shut, from the fact that I looked like I just fought [boxer] Mike Tyson. . . . I nearly died. That's the best thing that can happen to a rapper."

So with his jaw wired shut, West returned to the recording studio to sing on a regular basis until he was satisfied with his debut release. One song in particular, "Through the Wire," was the first track of several singles on *The College Dropout* to become a raging hit. The song chronicles West's ordeal. The album itself, which was released in 2004, went multiplatinum, selling 2.6 million copies. "The best thing is being able to get my creative ideas out," West told *Ebony*. "That's why I rap in the first place—so my voice can be heard."

The College Dropout was hailed as one of the best albums of the year. Critics praised West for taking hip-hop in a new direction. Songs on the album focus on walking with God while trying to "be real," and the producer/rapper says it all with a gospel choir backing him up. Hip-hop violinist Miri Ben-Ari worked with West on the album. Ben-Ari told *Ebony,* "He has a vision for things, for example, to bring live instrumentalists back to the game and create music like they did back in the day. Kanye is very open to new things; he is not afraid to think differently, to take a chance and to say his thoughts out loud."

An interview on *UniversalUrban.com* called West "one of a precious few rappers with actually something to say in his songs." West admits to writing lyrics on topics that aren't usually covered in rap music. "It's like if you wanna rap like Jay [Jay-Z], it's hard to rap like Jay and not rap about what Jay is rapping about," he told *UniversalUrban.* "Once I found out exactly how to rap about drugs and exactly how to rap about say no to drugs, I knew that I

Jay-Z, Jiggy, Jigga: A Star by Any Name

Jay-Z was born Shawn Carter on December 4, 1969. The Brooklyn-born boy was nicknamed Jazzy, which got shortened to the now-famous Jay-Z, which sometimes gets changed to Jiggy or Jigga. He is a man of many names and even more talent.

Jay-Z grew up in the dangerous Marcy Projects of Brooklyn. Before he hit his teens, Jay-Z's father left the family. Without a figurehead to support the family, Jay-Z hit the streets to find a way to support himself. He turned to selling drugs, a theme that makes its way into many of his songs. Jay-Z yearned to break into the rap industry and kept company with Big Jaz, a rapper with a record deal. Big Jaz taught the fledgling rapper the ins and outs of the music industry. Jay-Z got tired of waiting for someone to recognize his talent, so he made a bold move and established his own record company. With friends Damon Dash and Kareem "Biggs" Burke, he founded Roc-A-Fella Records, and in 1996 he released his debut album, *Reasonable Doubt.*

The album was unimpressive in terms of sales; it never got past number twenty-three on Billboard's album chart. But it is considered a classic among rap fans, and many call it his best work. The album spawned four hit singles, including "Feelin' It" and "Can't Knock the Hustle." Listeners of the album were rewarded with the sounds of R&B singer Mary J. Blige and rapper Notorious B.I.G. as well.

Jay-Z followed his debut with the 1997 release of *In My Lifetime, Vol. 1.* The album reached the number three spot on the charts and included contributions from rapper Puff Daddy and R&B singer/songwriter Teddy Riley. Unlike *Reasonable Doubt,* this album moved beyond the gangsta rap sound to appeal to the pop rap listening audience. Singles like "This City Is Mine" helped Jay-Z branch out and get airplay, which helped sales of the album. *Vol. 2: Hard Knock Life* followed the pop rap trend. The 1998 release contained radio-ready singles such as "Hard Knock Life" and "Can I Get A ... " The album increased his airtime as well as his popularity. Jay-Z had six singles off that one release.

Vol. 3: Life and Times of S. Carter was released in 1999. Nearly every single on this album featured a guest vocalist. The album was a huge hit among fans. Jay-Z began working with new producers for his next album, *Dynasty Roc la Familia.* The 2000 release included the Neptune's-produced single, "I Just Wanna Love U (Give It 2 Me)."

could fill the exact medium between that. Just think about whatever you've been through in the past week, and I have a song about that on my album."

Rewarded for his originality

West won four Billboard Music Awards in 2004: Male New Artist of the Year, New R&B/Hip-Hop Artist of the Year, R&B/Hip-Hop Producer of the Year, and Rap Artist of the Year.

The Blueprint was released in 2001, with producer/rapper Kanye West at the helm. Unlike his other albums, this one was mainly a solo effort. Many critics and fans consider *The Blueprint* to be Jay-Z's finest album. It featured one of the year's biggest hit single, "Izzo (H.O.V.A.)." The album helped West's career as well, cementing his reputation in the rap industry.

Jay-Z collaborated with the Roots for his *Unplugged* album in 2001. R. Kelly teamed up with the rapper for the 2002 album, *Best of Both Worlds.* That same year, Jay-Z released *The Blueprint 2: The Gift and the Curse.* In 2003, the rapper announced his retirement but promised one more album. That promise was fulfilled with the 2003 release of *The Black Album,* which claimed the number one spot on Billboard's album chart.

Although he is officially retired from the recording business, Jay-Z is far from done. He continues to make guest appearances on television music shows. In late July 2005 he appeared on *Jay-Z Live@Much.* The show was the latest in a series presented by MuchMusic, a Canadian music network. Jay-Z was joined by other Roc-A-Fella recording artists including Kanye West and pop-rock singing sensation Rihanna. Guests on the show performed a song or two and then sat for questions from the studio audience as well as callers who were watching the show on television. As co-owner of the Roc-A-Fella empire,

Jay-Z. © Tim Shaffer/Reuters/Corbis.

Jay-Z is kept busy with Rocawear, the company's clothing line and Roc-A-Fella films. He is co-owner of the New Jersey Nets basketball team as well as a New York sports bar called 40/40 Club. He is the first nonathlete to have a signature line of Reebok sneakers, called the S. Carter Collection. His shoe is the fastest-selling sneaker in Reebok's history.

West's debut album won Best Rap Album at the forty-seventh annual Grammy Awards in February 2005. The single "Jesus Walks" won Best Rap Song. And though he was nominated for Best New Artist, he lost to the pop/rock group **Maroon 5** (see entry). Altogether, West enjoyed ten Grammy nominations that year, either as producer or recording artist. He was not ignored for the Black Entertainment Television (BET) Awards, either. In fact, West walked away a double winner from the fifth annual awards in June 2005. He won Best Male Hip-Hop Artist and Video of the Year, for "Jesus Walks." West produced three different videos for that one song.

The popularity of even that one single ("Jesus Walks") is proof that West has found a niche for his gospel/rap/hip-hop/R&B style of music. But his tunes aren't without their critics. Barbara Kiviat of *Time* magazine asked the singer about the contradiction between the religious undertones of "Jesus Walks" and the profanity on the rest of *The College Dropout*. "Contradiction is part of who I am. I am a real person, and I make my mistakes and I laugh and I cry and I smile and I hate and I love," West replied. He also explained his commentary on college, which some critics say encourages kids to drop out. "People try to make it seem like if you go to college and you get all A's, that you'll move to the suburbs, have 2.5 kids and live happily ever after. But in many cases life just doesn't work like that.... What I'm saying is, Make your own decision."

Branching out

On July 2, thousands of recording artists donated their time and talent to Live 8, a concert held in ten cities and four continents across the globe. The mission of this free concert was to pressure political leaders into committing themselves to ending poverty in Africa. The concert was considered a huge success by all participants and its organizer, Bob Geldof (1954–).

West performed in Live 8 in Philadelphia, Pennsylvania, despite being threatened with a lawsuit if he did. The rapper told *MTV News,* "We had to go through a lot be here today. I had another performance and they're like, 'There's no way you can be here—you'll get sued if you go to this.'" West took the chance because he felt it was the least he could do to help out. "I would rather take that chance because it's important for my people," he told *MTV*.

As if life wasn't already busy enough, West has begun plans for his own line of clothing and sneakers, tentatively called Pastel and Mascott, respectively. A self-proclaimed fashion lover, the business mogul claims to have been compared to Carlton, the preppy and polite character from the television sitcom "The Fresh Prince of Bel-Air."

Kanye West performs at the 2005 Live 8 concert in Philadelphia. AP/Wide World Photos.

West established his own record label as well. G.O.O.D. (Getting Out Our Dreams) has already signed and released an album by John Legend (1979–), the label's first artist. West's second album, *Late Registration,* was released in August 2005. This was his first album made with his new production partner, film composer/musician/songwriter Jon Brion. His contributions to the album include playing guitar and keyboards as well as helping with song composition. The partnership surprised people in the music industry. Brion is best known for his orchestral arrangements for female artists Aimee Mann (1960–) and Fiona Apple (1977–). Other recording artists who collaborated with West on *Late Registration* include Jay-Z, Maroon 5's Adam Levine (1979–), and Brandy (1979–).

West's first single from the album, "Diamonds from Sierra Leone," received high marks from music critics. West wasn't so sure. The twenty eight year old told *Teen People,* "It's hard when people are depending on you to have an album that's not just good, but inspired. . . . I want my songs to touch people, to give them what they need. Every time I make an album, I'm trying to make a cure for cancer, musically. That stresses me out!"

West worked with award-winning video director Hype Williams to produce a video for "Diamonds." The singer used the video to raise awareness of the so-called "blood diamond" trade of Sierra Leone. Millions of Africans have lost their lives to the mining of these diamonds. The video positions the glamorous life depicted in a modern diamond commercial against the images of the brutal blood diamond trade. "I wanted to do whatever I could to learn more and educate people about the problem," West told *Business Wire*.

The song's lyrics speak for themselves:

Though it's thousands of miles away, Sierra Leone connect to what we go through today

Over here it's the drug trade, we die from drugs. Over there, they die from what we buy from drugs

The Diamonds. The chains, the bracelets, the charms is

I thought my Jesus piece was so harmless, till I seen a picture of a shorty armless, and here's the conflict

It's in the black person's soul, to rock that gold.

For More Information

Periodicals

Christian, Margena A. "Why everybody is talking about producer-turned-rapper Kanye West." *Jet* (January 31, 2005).

Davis, Kimberly. "Kanye West hip-hop's new big shot: talks about his next surprising moves and why marriage is the key to life." *Ebony* (April 2005).

Davis, Kimberly. "The many faces of Kanye West: producer-turned-hit rapper takes hip-hop in new direction." *Ebony* (June 2004).

Foxx, Jamie. "Kanye West: in just a few short years, he has emerged as one of music's premiere behind-the-scenes hitmakers. But it took a near-fatal crash—and one of the year's most inventive songs—for him to take center stage." *Interview* (August 2004).

"Kanye's Next Move." *Rolling Stone* (August 11, 2005): p. 16.

Kiviat, Barbara. "Ten Questions for Kanye West." *Time* (December 20, 2004).

"Throw Your Diamonds in the Sky: Kanye West Returns with Epic New Video 'Diamonds from Sierra Leone'; Hype Williams-Directed Video Set to Air This Week as Hot New Remix Feat. Jay-Z Blasts off at Radio." *Business Wire* (June 15, 2005).

Web Sites

Birchmeier, Jason. "Jay-Z." *MTV.com*. http://www.mtv.com/bands/az/jay_z/bio.jhtml (accessed on August 9, 2005).

"Kanye West." *Rapcityz.com*. http://www.rapcityz.com/biokanyewst.htm (accessed on August 9, 2005).

"Kanye West." *UniversalUrban.com*. http://universalurban.com/kanyewest/index.php (accessed on August 9, 2005).

"Kanye West: Biography." *VH1.com*. http://www.vh1.com/artists/az/west_kanye/bio.jhtml (accessed on August 9, 2005).

"Kanye West in Legal Battle to Appear at Live 8." *Femalefirst* (July 4, 2005). http://www.femalefirst.co.uk/entertainment/69392004.htm (accessed on August 9, 2005).

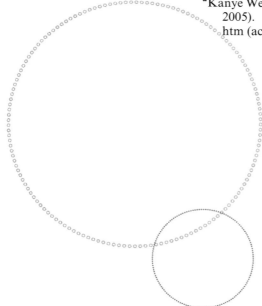

Christopher Wheeldon

Yeovil, Somerset, England

Ballet choreographer, dancer

Called ballet's hottest choreographer in 2004, Christopher Wheeldon has choreographed more than thirty ballets in five years. His productions have almost always received high marks from critics, and ballet companies across the country consider it an honor to work with the thirty two year old. Wheeldon has been compared to ballet masters George Balanchine (1904–1983) and Jerome Robbins (1918–1998) almost since he began choreographing. And that comparison has never left him.

Born to dance

Christopher Wheeldon was born in Somerset, England. He began lessons at the East Coker Ballet School when he was eight years old. He enrolled in London's Royal Ballet School at age eleven and trained until he was eighteen. And though he was a dancer in those early days, hints of his future as a choreographer shone through. "I enjoyed being the center of attention, being bossy," Wheeldon told Sarah Kaufman of the *Washington Post*. While home during summer vacation, the young dancer would recruit neighborhood friends into dance productions he wrote and choreographed.

While still a student, Wheeldon won prizes for his choreography. At seventeen, he was one of five dancers chosen to compete at the Prix de Lausanne, an international dance competition held each year to help dance students kickstart their professional careers. One

"Dance has been my way of life since I was a child and I'll never give it up—it really is my reason for living."

hundred and twenty dancers are chosen to compete; only fifteen make the final round. The winner is awarded a study scholarship with the finest schools and dance companies in the world. Wheeldon won the Gold Medal in 1991. That same year, he was accepted into the Royal Ballet Company (RBC).

Wheeldon stayed with the RBC for just two years. Then an unusual opportunity presented itself. While recovering from a dance injury in 1993, Wheeldon was lying on his sofa with a bag of frozen peas on his ankle to keep the swelling down, watching endless hours of television. A commercial played that promised a free plane ticket to New York City for everyone who bought a Hoover vacuum. Wheeldon bought the Hoover and claimed his ticket. He visited the New York City Ballet (NYCB) during his trip and participated in a couple of classes as a guest. Even before leaving the city to return home, Wheeldon was invited to become a member of their company. The twenty year old accepted and was promoted to the rank of Soloist in 1998. During his years as a dancer, Wheeldon worked with some of the most famous choreographers of all time, including Jerome Robbins and George Balanchine. Years later, his innate feel for choreography and his willingness to reimagine and rework traditional ballets would be favorably compared to these dance masters.

Finds his calling as a choreographer

Although he enjoyed dancing, Wheeldon never forgot the advice given to him by Sir Kenneth MacMillan, a respected British ballet choreographer who had more than forty ballets under his belt by the time he retired. Wheeldon shared with John Percival of *The Independent,* "I was summoned to the presence, and he told me, 'You seem to have some talent for choreography; you should take every opportunity you have to practice it and make ballets'." Wheeldon did as he was told and choreographed student-led productions for the Royal Ballet School, the London Studio Centre, and the School of American Ballet. He proved himself capable of working with large ballet corps (groups), a talent that set him apart from other young choreographers.

Wheeldon quit dancing at the end of the spring season in 2000 to focus his attention and energy on choreography. Peter Martins, director of the NYCB, hired Wheeldon to be the company's first artist in residence, a position created just for him. Wheeldon was just twenty-eight years old. His first chor-eographed ballet as resident artist was *Polyphonia.* It was given its world premiere in January 2001 and received excellent reviews. Clive Barnes of *Dance Magazine* wrote, "There is not a step in *Polyphonia* that doesn't progress naturally from the step before it. The dance—prickly, angular—moves with the force of nature like the wind." Jackie McGlone of *scotsman.com* called the ballet an "immaculate masterpiece." Wheeldon won the London Critics' Circle Award for Best New Ballet for *Polyphonia.* A production in 2002 by the NYCB earned the Olivier Award for Best New Dance Production.

In May 2001, the NYCB performed Wheeldon's *Variations Serieuses.* With that ballet, Wheeldon appeared to have earned the respect of even the toughest critics. Anna Kisselgoff, dean of

Christopher Wheeldon, pictured here in 1995, quit dancing in 2000 to focus his attention and energy on choreography. © Julie Lemberger/Corbis.

American dance critics, wrote in the *New York Times,* "No ballet choreographer of his generation can match his imaginative use of the classical vocabulary." And that is what the budding choreographer became known for: his ability to modernize the classical ballet without sacrificing its strength and beauty. Wheeldon credited his training. "I feel quite lucky and grateful for growing up in the environment of theatrical story ballets and a very solid, very old tradition in ballet," he was quoted as saying in 2001. That same May, Wheeldon was named resident choreographer for NYCB, another position created just for him.

A man of many projects

While choreographing ballets for the NYCB, Wheeldon had his creative hands in projects for other organizations, including the Boston Ballet, the Royal Ballet, and the San Francisco Ballet. He won countless awards for his many ballets, and more than one New York critic called him "the best thing to happen to ballet for 50 years." Wheeldon admits to not believing his own publicity. He explained his stance to Jackie McGlone of *scotsman.com:* "I simply do not set too much store by the good reviews, because then I don't have to set too much by the bad ones."

Wheeldon got his first taste of bad publicity with his Broadway debut ballet, *The Sweet Smell of Success.* The 2002 ballet was a stage adaptation of a film by the same name. Without exception, the musical is considered Wheeldon's weakest work. Critic Gerald Rabkin wrote a review for *Culture Vulture.com* in which he called Wheeldon's choreography "merely serviceable," meaning it did the job but was nothing to get excited about. Wheeldon's debut was not without value, however, as it introduced him to actor and writer John Lithgow, who performed in the musical. Their next collaboration (in *Carnival of the Animals*) was considered more successful.

By June 2002, Wheeldon had produced the ballet *Morphoses.* He followed that up with several projects, including a 2003 ballet set to the score (music) of Camille Saint-Saens' *Carnival of the Animals.* The ballet was given the same title and included verse written by Lithgow.

The year 2002 brought Wheeldon together professionally with Scottish composer James MacMillan. The two ballet greats collaborated on *Tryst,* performed by the Royal Ballet Company. MacMillan was thrilled at the opportunity to work with Wheeldon. In an interview for *Ballet Magazine* in 2003, the composer reminisced, "He has shone a light into the music, which is a new and unexpected perspective. There is something in both our work that evokes this sense of mysticism, mystery or otherness. I was aware of that corresponding sense of beauty ... [which] allowed me to revisit the music of *Tryst* and see again how vivid the experience was when I wrote the music initially 14 years ago." *Tryst* was just one of a number of Wheeldon/ MacMillan projects performed by the RBC.

Swan Lake

In 2004, Wheeldon was commissioned (hired) by the Pennsylvania Ballet to choreograph a ballet of his choice. Wheeldon chose one of his favorite ballets, *Swan Lake,* and was given $1 million to make it happen. He was indecisive about how to proceed with the project. Should he go the traditional route and perform the entire (and very long) ballet? Or would it be better to modernize the production a bit, putting a new spin on the narrative?

In the end, the reviews spoke for themselves. Janet Anderson of the *Philadelphia City Paper* praised Wheeldon's inventiveness. "The choreographer managed the impossible, keeping all the classic's famous moments and yet creating something magnificently, even wildly, original for Pennsylvania Ballet." Wheeldon incorporated different performance styles into his *Swan Lake* production. While keeping the choreography traditional, he updated the sets and costumes and incorporated a modern energy into the classic.

According to *Dancing Times* magazine, Wheeldon had concerns about his approach to the ballet. "I always felt Philadelphia was a fairly conservative audience, not just for ballet and dance. I was a little concerned that this might be too much of a stretch for them but, as it turned out, almost across the board, people not only accepted it but enthusiastically embraced it." The ballet was so successful that Wheeldon was invited to take the production to the 2005 Edinburgh International Festival in Scotland. This was a monumental moment for the Pennsylvania Ballet, an organization that had kept a low profile over the years in comparison to troupes such as the New York City Ballet. All ballet companies aspire to be invited to the festival; to receive an

The Late, Great Jerome Robbins

When Chris Wheeldon is compared to Jerome Robbins, the young choreographer takes that as a compliment. Wheeldon studied with Robbins in the early stages of his career. The budding choreographer was just nineteen years old when he danced his first workshop with Robbins. The master punched Wheeldon on the shoulders and muttered "Mmmm—not bad!" As Wheeldon told *Ballet* magazine in 2003, "He was a far more generous man than people give him credit for. That little punch—because he didn't have to say anything—was enough for me to give me the boost that I needed."

Jerome Robbins was born October 11, 1918, in New York City. He dropped out of college when he realized his limited potential as a student and found work training as a ballet dancer at the Sandor Dance School. In 1944, Robbins tried his hand at writing a ballet, and his first, *Fancy Free,* opened at the Metropolitan Opera House in April that year. The ballet received twenty-four curtain calls; Robbins was an instant hit. He had teamed up with the then-unknown composer Leonard Bernstein (1918–1990), who wrote the score for the musical. The team produced another hit in December. *On the Town* cemented Robbins's place in ballet history, and—with 66 ballets to his credit—he remained the master of his craft until his death more than fifty years later.

Robbins enjoyed particular success with his Broadway titles, including *West Side Story* (another Bernstein-Robbins smash hit). His role in this production won him two Academy Awards (one for direction, one for choreography), but this was also the point in his career in which he earned a reputation as being a ruthless perfectionist. It was a reputation that would be with him throughout his life.

Jerome Robbins (left) with famous actor/dancer Gene Kelly.
AP/Wide World Photos.

Regardless of reputation, Robbins's style paid off. The choreographer won countless awards for his work throughout his career, and his name is attached to such famous musicals as *Fiddler on the Roof* and *Gypsy.* In 1998, Robbins died in his home from a stroke at the age of seventy-nine.

Robbins is largely credited, along with George Balanchine (1904–1983) and Lincoln Kirstein (1906–1996), with establishing the New York City Ballet. Kirstein, who supported the arts through his financial donations, helped fund and bring to life Balanchine's vision of a ballet school. Once the American School of Ballet was established, Robbins and Balanchine set out to make the New York City Ballet the most renowned ballet company in the world.

invitation is basically to be told you've made it to the big-time. Wheeldon had been to the festival in 2003 with the San Francisco Ballet, where the troupe performed *Rush*. For that production, Wheeldon won the coveted National Dance Award for Best Choreography in 2004.

2005 and beyond

Since 2000, Wheeldon has created more than thirty new productions, though he lost track of the exact count. In early 2005, the award-winning choreographer worked with the NYCB to create *After the Rain,* his eleventh ballet with the company. The ballet was meant to be a swan song (the last performance) for veteran ballet dancer Jock Soto, who was on the verge of retiring. *After the Rain* garnered high praise for both Wheeldon and Soto. Wheeldon also pleased critics with his *American in Paris* and *There Where She Loved.*

By mid-July 2005, the choreographer was spending his time with the San Francisco Ballet, working on his new production, *Quarternary*. The name means "four parts;" each act of the ballet focuses on a specific season in the cycle. Wheeldon loves the San Francisco Ballet dancers. "They're quick," he told Rachel Howard of the *San Francisco Chronicle*. "There's no waiting while someone sulks because they don't like the steps."

The thirty-two-year-old Wheeldon lives in New York's Upper West Side and enjoys a second home in Spain. He keeps his private life private, but doesn't mind talking about his work. In his 2005 interview with Jackie McGlone, the master craftsman mused, "I sometimes wonder if I'm going to fail the next time, and indeed whether there's going to be a next time. Perhaps that's why I feel that the time has come to take a step in another direction. And I will; I will."

For More Information

Periodicals

Carman, Joseph. "The Evolution of Christopher Wheeldon." *Dance Magazine* (May 1, 2003).

Kaufman, Sarah. "Ever on Their Toes." *Washington Post* (February 24, 2005): p. C01.

Mead, David. "Edinburgh Festival Preview: Pennsylvania Ballet in Wheeldon's *Swan Lake*." *Dancing Times* (July 2007).

Percival, John. "Dance: Sweet Success." *The Independent* (May 6, 2002).

Porterfield, Christopher. "In the Ear, Out the Foot: A forward-looking traditionalist, Christopher Wheeldon, 31, is ballet's hottest choreographer." *Time* (May 10, 2004).

Web Sites

Anderson, Janet. "Swan Lake." *Philadelphia Citypaper.net* (June 10–16, 2004). http://citypaper.net/articles/2004-06-10/dance.shtml (accessed on August 9, 2005).

"Christopher Wheeldon: new ballet." *Royal Opera House* (February 12, 2005). http://info.royaloperahouse.org/News/Index.cfm?ccs = 714 (accessed on August 9, 2005).

"Christopher Wheeldon, Resident Choreographer of New York City Ballet." *New York City Ballet*. http://www.nycballet.com/about/cwheeldon.html (accessed on August 9, 2005).

Howard, Rachel. "Christopher Wheeldon is taking S.F. Ballet to choreography's cutting edge—and to Paris." *SFGate.com* (July 1, 2005). http://www.sfgate.com/cgi-bin/article.cgi?file = /c/a/2005/07/01/DDG9PDEKHG18.DTL (accessed on August 9, 2005).

McCarthy, Brendan. "Christopher Wheeldon, Choreographer." *Ballet.co Magazine* (August 2003). http://www.ballet.co.uk/magazines/yr_03/aug03/interview_wheeldon.htm (accessed on August 9, 2005).

McGlone, Jackie. "Leap of Faith." *Scotsman.com* (July 17, 2005). http://news.scotsman.com/features.cfm?id = 1635022005 (accessed August 9, 2005).

Vaill, Amanda. "A Biography in Brief." *Jerome Robbins*. http://jeromerobbins.org/bio-vaill.htm (accessed on August 9, 2005).

Wood, Astrida. "Chris Wheeldon Shines in 'After the Rain'." *Show Business Weekly* (January 26, 2005). http://www.showbusinessweekly.com/archive/318/dance.shtml (accessed on August 9, 2005).

Viktor Yushchenko

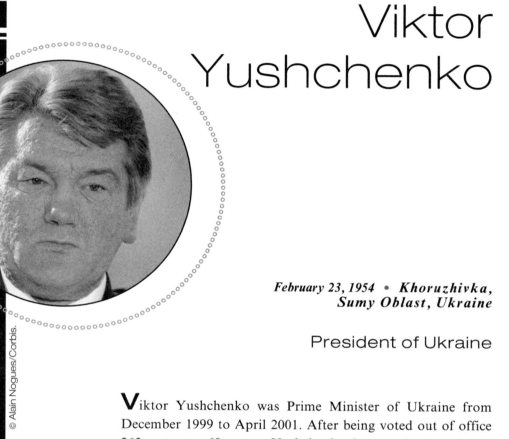

© Alain Nogues/Corbis.

February 23, 1954 • *Khoruzhivka, Sumy Oblast, Ukraine*

President of Ukraine

Viktor Yushchenko was Prime Minister of Ukraine from December 1999 to April 2001. After being voted out of office 263 votes to 69 votes, Yushchenko became leader of Our Ukraine, a political coalition (a combination of people working for the same cause). Members of Our Ukraine won 101 seats in the 450-seat legislature in 2002, making Our Ukraine the most powerful party in Parliament (Ukraine's governing body). In 2004 Yushchenko was elected the president of Ukraine in the country's first free election. During his campaign, he was poisoned with a near-fatal dose of the toxin dioxin. The poisoning has left him with permanent scars on his face. This personal attack left Yushchenko even more determined to lead his country out of the state of government and police corruption it has been living in for decades.

Helps establish Europe's newest bank

Viktor Andriyovych Yushchenko was born to a teacher's family on February 23, 1954, in the village of Khoruzhivka in Sumy Oblast, Ukraine. (Ukraine is in eastern Europe and borders the Black Sea.)

Yushchenko graduated college in 1975 from the Ternopil Finance and Economics Institute. His first job was with the Union of Soviet Socialist Republics (USSR) State Bank, where he was an economist and department chief. After earning his graduate

> "I am not afraid of anything or anybody."

degree in finance and credit from the Ukrainian Institute of Economics and Agricultural Management in 1984, Yushchenko was appointed Deputy Director for Agricultural Crediting for the Ukraine branch of the USSR State Bank. He held this position until 1987, when he left for another banking position elsewhere.

The National Bank of Ukraine (NBU) hired Yushchenko to be its governor (president) in 1993. NBU was Europe's newest central bank at the time, and Yushchenko played an important role in developing its policies and procedures. He stayed with NBU for six years.

Earns international reputation as Prime Minister

In December 1999 Ukraine's president, Leonid Kuchma, nominated Yushchenko as prime minister. In this case, a prime minister is the person responsible for carrying out the president's orders and directives. It is an important job. Parliament approved Yushchenko's nomination 296 to 12.

Yushchenko brought to life a number of reforms that helped turn around Ukraine's struggling economy. He is credited with paying off millions of dollars of Ukrainian debt through cuts in federal spending and by improving investment conditions in the country and overseas. Because of his success, Yushchenko was able to restore public trust in government, something that was destroyed through years of political corruption. One of the more challenging aspects of Yushchenko's job was to increase the level of honesty and open communication between the government and the public. Prior to his election, Ukraine lived in fear of its government leaders, who were infamous for their willingness to stop at nothing to get what they wanted.

In 2001, Yushchenko's deputy prime minister, Yulia Tymoshenko (1960–), got into a heated argument with leaders of the coal-mining and natural gas industries. These leaders were powerful and had great influence on an already-corrupt government. As a result, parliament voted to remove Yushchenko from office, 263 to 69. Though a harsh response, this move did not come as a great surprise to anyone. The government in Ukraine was mainly Communist; it believed in a powerful governing body that gave citizens few choices in anything ranging from food to healthcare. This is called a centralized government. Yushchenko believed in democracy and capitalism: He wanted people to be able to own businesses and enjoy the freedoms that America is known for. His beliefs threatened those few powerful men in Ukraine's government.

Four million votes were gathered in support of a petition to get Yushchenko back in office. Tens of thousands of Ukrainians protested his dismissal. Their efforts were of no use; Yushchenko was out of office. But he was not out of power.

Our Ukraine

Early in 2002 Viktor Yushchenko became the leader of Our Ukraine, a political coalition. Our Ukraine united various democratic parties and groups from across the nation in hopes of bringing democracy to the Ukraine. Our Ukraine formed the largest parliamentary faction of 2002, claiming 101 seats of the 450-seat legislature. It seemed the corrupt government of Ukraine was in danger of being overthrown.

Although Ukraine's presidents were determined by election, it was no secret that fraud was widespread in elections. Everyone knew it, and no one felt able to fight it with even a remote hope of winning. Yushchenko changed that. When he announced he would run for the office of president in the 2004 election, Yushchenko brought hope to hundreds of thousands of citizens who were weary of living under a dictatorship disguised as a presidency. They were ready for a change.

Becomes victim of a murder plot

Yushchenko was running against Prime Minister Viktor Yanukovych. Yanukovych was a political ally of outgoing president Leonid Kuchma. Kuchma's administration depended upon corruption and dishonesty for its power. Government officials ruled with a sense of terror rather than justice. For the powerful and wealthy few, having Yanukovych elected president was important. Should Yushchenko win, Ukraine's government was sure to topple. Yushchenko's campaign promises included a better quality of life for Ukrainians through democracy. His wife, Katherine, told CBS in a 2005 interview, "He was a great threat to the old system, where there was a great deal of corruption, where people were making millions, if not billions."

On September 6, 2004, Yushchenko became ill after dining with leaders of the Ukrainian secret police. Unlike other social or political engagements, this dinner did not include anyone else on Yushchenko's team. No precautions were taken regarding the food. Within hours after the dinner, Yushchenko began vomiting violently. His face became paralyzed; he could not speak or read. He developed a severe stomachache and backache as well as gastrointestinal pain. Outwardly, Yushchenko developed what is known as chloracne, a serious skin condition that leaves the face scarred and disfigured.

By December 2004, doctors had determined that Yushchenko had been the victim of dioxin poisoning. Dioxin is a name given to a group of related toxins that can cause cancer and even death. Dioxin was used in the biochemical weapon called Agent Orange during the Vietnam War (1954–75; a

Viktor Yushchenko photographed in March 2002, left, and December 2004, right. Toxicological analysis found the mysterious illness that scarred his face was caused by dioxin poisoning. AP/Wide World Photos.

controversial war in which the United States aided South Vietnam in its fight against a takeover by Communist North Vietnam). Yushchenko had a dioxin level six thousand times greater than that normally found in the bloodstream. His is the second-highest level ever recorded.

Yushchenko immediately suspected he had been poisoned, though Kuchma's camp passionately denied such allegations. Instead, when Yushchenko showed up at a parliamentary meeting shortly after the poisoning incident, Kuchma's men teased him, saying he must have had too much to drink or was out too late the night before.

Dioxin can stay in the body for up to thirty-five years. Experts predict that his swelling and scars will fade but never completely disappear. John Henry, a toxicologist at London's Imperial Hospital, told *RedNova.com,* "It'll be a couple of years, and he will always be a bit pockmarked. After damage as heavy as that, I think he will not return to his film star looks." And Yushchenko will live with the constant threat of cancer.

At first it was believed the poison must have come from a Russian laboratory. Russia was a strong supporter of Kuchma and lobbied against Yushchenko in the 2004 election. But by July 2005, Yushchenko's security forces were able to trace the poison to a lab in Ukraine. Though not entirely ruling out Russia's involvement, Yushchenko is quoted on his Web site as saying "I'm sure that even though some people are running from the investigation, we will get them. I am not afraid of anything or anybody."

Birth of a revolution

Even an attempt on his life didn't stop Yushchenko from finishing his presidential campaign. On October 31, 2004, neither Yushchenko nor Yanukovych won the absolute majority of votes (meaning no candidate received more than 50 percent of the votes). Ukrainian law mandates that in such an event, the two candidates with the highest number of votes must compete in a run-off election. The winner of that election would officially become president. That election took place on November 21, 2004, in Kiev, the Ukraine capital.

Exit polls (the unofficial tally of votes at the end of an election) on November 21 showed that Yushchenko had an 11 percent lead over Yanukovych. Official results gave the election to Yanukovych by a mere 3 percent. Official votes were counted by officials under the authority of Yanukovych. The incumbent laid the blame for the difference on the media's shoulders. But Yushchenko's team countered by publicizing obvious evidence of electoral fraud on the part of the government, which backed Yanukovych. Signs of similar fraud were apparent in the original election held in October, too, but to a much lesser—and more difficult to prove—extent.

The Ukrainian people had had enough. Hundreds of thousands of protesters gathered in Kiev and other cities across Ukraine. Yushchenko supporters planned strikes and sit-ins to protest the obvious rigging of the run-off election. They wore orange ribbons, carried orange banners, and wore orange clothing. Orange had been the official color of Yushchenko's campaign. Thus, the Orange Revolution was born.

The Orange Revolution brought Ukraine's political crisis to the attention of the entire world. Ukraine's Supreme Court demanded another run-off election be held. Voters gathered together once again, and this time, the results were clear. Viktor Yushchenko was declared the official winner and was sworn into office on January 23, 2005, in Kiev. He became the country's first freely elected president.

After the final election, the *New York Times* reported that Ukrainian security agencies helped the Orange Revolution succeed. Remember, these agencies were under the authority of the corrupt president and his favored candidate, Yanukovych. The paper reported that on November 28, more than ten thousand troops were ordered to put down the Orange Revolution protests in Kiev. The commander of the military unit warned Yushchenko's team of the crackdown, thereby giving them time to alert the protesters and avoid bloodshed. Further revelations show that many intelligence officers supported Yushchenko's ideas of democracy and gathered proof of voting fraud and incriminating conversations held between leaders of Yanukovych's team. It is believed that this evidence was recorded and provided to Yushchenko by Ukrainian Security Services.

After his official election with a 51.99 percent of the vote, Yushchenko addressed the crowd: "This is a victory of the Ukrainian people, the Ukrainian nation.... This is what dozens of millions of Ukrainians dreamt about. Today it is fashionable, stylish and beautiful to be a citizen of Ukraine." And at 3:00 AM on December 27, he addressed his supporters with "during 14 years we were independent, but we were not free," as reported in the *Ukrainian Weekly*.

Pledges membership of Ukraine to European Union

The European Union (EU) is a network for economic and political cooperation between twenty-five countries. These European states

Viktor Yushchenko waves to supporters during a ceremony to mark his inauguration in Kiev, Ukraine, January 23, 2005.
© Baran Alexander/ITAR-TASS/Corbis.

joined together in an effort to establish rules and regulations of trade, labor, and business that would make for a more stable economy. In the past, Ukraine was indifferent to the EU; it wanted no part in the framework. Instead, president Kuchma favored privatization of the Ukrainian economy, which meant giving all the power to a handful of people who had pledged their support to Kuchma. Yushchenko recognized the benefits that belonging to the EU would provide his country. In an article on his official Web site, Yushchenko said, "The citizens of no European country object to Ukraine joining the EU. We consider that Ukraine is an inseparable part of Europe."

Although Russian president Vladimir Putin (1952–) gave his support to the opposition, Yushchenko held a series of high-profile meetings with the leader in 2005. Political experts expected progress in all areas that once were deadlocked under the old leadership. Already by July 2005, Russia was exporting more goods to Ukraine than ever before. The key to improving relations with Europe and joining with full membership in the EU is Ukraine's relationship with Russia. Russia is a political and economic powerhouse, and Yushchenko was not the president Putin was hoping to deal with.

Six months later

Six months after Yushchenko's victory, supporters of Yanukovych lined the streets in protest. Some were so angry that they quit their jobs and lived on the streets full time. These protesters claimed that anyone who supported the opposition was being persecuted. Yanukovych has been questioned by the police many times, and the Ukrainian Ombudsman (person who works with people who have a complaint) said it was investigating the cases of twelve thousand workers who said they were fired because they did not support Yushchenko in the election.

The Minister of Justice denied that anyone was being politically persecuted. He told BBC News that authorities were investigating allegations of corruption because to do otherwise would be a violation of the spirit of the Orange Revolution. "People were demanding justice."

There is no doubt Yushchenko was making drastic and sweeping changes. July 18, 2005, was a particularly busy day for the president. He dismissed the leaders of all regional interior departments. The president told leaders at a meeting of Interior Ministry officials, "Trust in police must be restored. This is our common work, which must begin from replacing the local police heads."

That same day, Yushchenko ordered a decree to be drawn up that would disband Ukraine's traffic police department. After deciding it was impossible to rid the department of deep-seated corruption, the president announced he would abolish the department altogether, leaving twenty-three thousand employees out of work. Traffic police in Ukraine are known for their habit of stopping motorists and fining them on the spot for imaginary offenses. They are infamous for demanding bribe money.

Yushchenko claimed that he warned senior officials three times that if the department did not clean itself up, he would get rid of it. The new patrol service would be closely monitored for bribe-taking and swearing. Yushchenko told law enforcement officials, "You are servants of the state. Try to talk without swearing. If anyone can't learn to do this, then write a letter of resignation."

Scandal at the top

In July 2005, Yushchenko's nineteen-year-old son, Andriy, became embroiled in a scandal that infuriated Ukrainians, regardless of their political convictions. Journalists brought to light Andriy's lavish lifestyle and questioned the morality of such a lifestyle in a country that is still struggling to find its way. According to *Mosnews.com,* the young Yushchenko drives a brand new BMW 16 (valued at $120,000), uses a platinum body Vertu mobile phone (priced at $30,000), and bribes restaurants with wads of cash to give him the best tables. These facts alone are not unusual when talking about the children of political leaders; many children of leaders worldwide live lives of luxury. But in this case, the problem stems from where the money comes. Nikolai Katerinchuk, Ukraine's deputy head of the country's tax inspectorate, claims Andriy's annual income amounts to $100 million. And that money comes from the sale of Orange Revolution memorabilia.

After Yushchenko's election victory, the president gave his son all property rights for Orange Revolution memorabilia. The items are still popular and enjoy steady sales in the region of Kiev. A flag sells for $1-$5; a T-shirt costs $20. According to a 2005 Russian News and Information Agency article written by political commentator Peter Lavelle, when asked about his son's spending habits, the president replied, "Let me tell you, friends, such . . . [questions] should be humiliating for an honest journalist." Yushchenko has been highly criticized for his emotional response to his son's predicament. Many citizens see his reaction as symbolic of all that is wrong since the Orange Revolution.

Lavelle considered Yushchenko's comments to be the same as an admission of how little has been done to deal with corrupt government officials since Yushchenko took office. Ukrainian citizens are very aware that some state officials continue to live well at the expense of everyone else. This is seen as a breach of just one of the promises made by the Orange Revolution.

Murder and mayhem

To make matters worse for Yushchenko, frustration levels of the public were already high due to the lack of justice for murdered journalist Georgy Gongadze. Thirty-one-year-old Gongadze was the respected publisher of the online journal *Ukrainska Pravda,* a publication known for its willingness to print the truth even if it angered people in powerful positions. He was considered a hero for the underdog, a champion of justice in the midst of evil. The journalist went missing on November 13, 2000. He was found beheaded in a ditch some time later in a suburb of Kiev. At the time of his death, Gongadze had been investigating government corruption in Ukraine. Since Gongadze's murder, two more journalists have been killed.

Although an investigation got underway, no satisfactory results have been publicized. Yushchenko had promised citizens that the case would reach the courts by May 2005. As of August that year, his pledge went unfulfilled. Yushchenko has been criticized for hiring incompetent lawyers, and it is considered fact that Kuchma had been buying off people in the case whose knowledge might help solve the crime. It is widely suspected that Kuchma ordered the journalist's kidnapping and murder, but no progress seemed to have been made in proving that allegation. Yushchenko was being held accountable for that lack of progress and justice in the Gongadze murder. Failure to close the case was damaging the president's legitimacy, as well as those who serve under him. The hopes that fueled the Orange Revolution have been seriously dimmed.

For More Information

Web Sites

Fawkes, Helen. "Protest camps badger Yushchenko." *BBC News* (July 18, 2005). http://news.bbc.co.uk/go/pr/fr/-/2/hi/europe/4693419.stm (accessed on August 9, 2005).

Lavelle, Peter. "Yushchenko loses his Orange Revolution cool." *Russian News and Information Agency Novosti* (July 27, 2005). http://en.rian.ru/analysis/20050727/40985857.html (accessed on August 9, 2005).

Mite, Valentinas. "Ukraine: Has Yushchenko's Political Honeymoon Come to an End?" *Radio Free Europe/Radio Liberty* (July 27, 2005). http://www.rferl.org/featuresarticle/2005/07/6ed958c8-e9ab-4781-9aeb-3664aea0b123.html (accessed on August 9, 2005).

Nynka, Andrew. "Yushchenko elected president of Ukraine." *Ukrainian Weekly* (January 2, 2005). http://www.ukrweekly.com/Archive/2005/010501.shtml (accessed on August 9, 2005).

President of Ukraine: Official Web Site. http://www.president.gov.ua/en/ (accessed on August 9, 2005).

"Profile: Viktor Yushchenko." *BBC News* (January 1, 2005). http://news.bbc.co.uk/go/pr/fr/-/2/hi/europe/4035789.stm (accessed on August 9, 2005).

"Ukraine disappoints the West." *Pravda.ru* (July 28, 2005). http://english.pravda.ru/world/20/92/370/15875_Ukraine.html (accessed on August 9, 2005).

"Ukraine traffic police abolished." *BBC News* (July 18, 2005). http://news.bbc.co.uk/2/hi/europe/4694199.stm (accessed on August 9, 2005).

"Viktor Yushchenko." *Biography.ms.* http://victor-yushchenko.biography.ms/ (accessed on August 9, 2005).

"Yushchenko: 'Live and Carry On'." *CBSNews.com* (January 30, 2005). http://www.cbsnews.com/stories/2005/01/28/60minutes/main670103.shtml (accessed on August 9, 2005).

"Yushchenko poisoned by most harmful dioxin." *MSNBC.com* (December 17, 2004). http://www.msnbc.msn.com/id/6697752/ (accessed on August 9, 2005).

"Yushchenko Poisoned, Doctors Say." *DW-World.DE Deutsche welle* (December 11, 2004). http://www.dw-world.de/dw/article/0,1564,1425561,00.html (accessed on August 9, 2005).

Yushchenko, Viktor. "Our Ukraine." *Opinion Journal* (December 3, 2004). http://www.opinionjournal.com/editorial/feature.html?id = 110005974 (accessed August 9, 2005).

Volume numbers are in italic; **boldface** *indicates main entries and their page numbers; (ill.) following a page number indicates an illustration on the page.*

C

h

S

t